IN PURSUIT...

The Search For Absolute Truth & Peace

By

Daryl B. Detherage, PhD

In Pursuit...

COPYRIGHT PAGE

Preface

THINK! That is the preface for this book. Take that plunge into the unforeseen... independent thought and study, but be prepared to take the necessary actions! Faith requires action, TODAY, not good intentions for tomorrow.

People have allowed incorrect media, music, and the confused separation of politics and religion to shape our beliefs into a stir pot of melted mass individualism. Yet that individualism is a mass-mentality at its base, thereby growing a herded culture of open-mindedness and wide-acceptance of very twisted and perverted beliefs where adherence to those principles that our country was founded upon are now perceived as religious imprisonment, rather than the freedom that allowed us to form a separate nation.

Think for yourself! Start your pursuit for Truth & Peace in the right place, lose the false hopes of salvation and research some truth for yourself. Determine your own path, the right path, based upon your own study of the Bible, at least the validity of using biblical principles in your life; your own research of the undisputed most documented account of historical truths, and define your own beliefs.

In Pursuit…

Think… and take back **control of your own eternal future.**

The game of life is the game of boomerangs. Our thoughts, deeds, and words return to us sooner or later, with astounding accuracy.
Lesson: Aim before you act or this is gonna hurt!

Dedication

This book is first dedicated to a purpose, rather than to a person or small group of persons. The purpose is to serve others and reach out to everyone and to inspire and motivate all who read this book to think. The purpose is greater than me or any single individual, yet if only one person responds and grows from the words herein and begins to truly study the Bible, all of my efforts in this will be fruitful and worth every second devoted to its writing.

The purpose is best defined in **Colossians 2: 2 & 3** – *"that their hearts may be encouraged, having been knit together in love, and attaining to all the wealth that comes from the full assurance of understanding, resulting in a true knowledge of God's mystery, that is, Christ Himself, in whom are hidden all the treasures of wisdom and knowledge."*

Secondly, I dedicate this book to my father who left the troubles of this world behind and has begun his journey in spirit, at the age of 80; and to my mother, who has always remained steadfast and pure. Both have been an inspiration and living testimony to the Truth of the Bible.

God takes those home whom He can no longer love from a distance.

In Pursuit…
My Dad is at home. He was promoted to Heaven on January 31, 2009.
His legacy to us is in our knowing God.

Dad ran the race, and finished the race with honor exemplified towards his God and Father. Now we have the challenge of finishing that same race, and the hope and promise of receiving that same reward.

As Christians, we celebrate that day! This is exactly what we are all hoping for… to finish the race, to have our Leader call us out of duty from the spiritual warfare we are in everyday and send us home, to tell us that we have served with honor, as Dad did, and tell us **"Rest, weary soldier. You have fought the good fight and defeated the enemy, good and faithful servant. Come home."**
To a soldier of Christ, good & faithful servant to God, my Dad, my Best Friend, my Hero; & my Mom, the finest example I know of Christian purity.

Table of Contents

In Pursuit…

1 –The Foundation

Are you perfectly happy and content with everything in your life right now? If you are, then please return this book and begin writing your own. It's guaranteed to be a Best Seller! However, if you are among the rest of us who are still striving, I believe that you will enjoy, gain some awareness, knowledge, inspiration, and practical lessons from the dynamics of this book. Understand from the onset, the subjects studied and presented herein are not intended to be exhaustive all-inclusive research studies, but only enough to start you thinking, questioning, and studying on your own with enough information to start making informed intelligent decisions.

To achieve this, we must begin to break through that societal mindset of mass acceptance and confusion, and begin focusing your thoughts towards free-thinking, and open your mind to the possibility of a single unified absolute Truth that you can make the basis of your decision-making.

Now, let's establish the foundational integrity of this book right from the start. The foundation of the thoughts, ideas, concepts, and guiding principles of this entire book are based upon the Bible. You may admire that, or you may be ready to close and throw

In Pursuit...

this book away right now, based on that last statement, but WAIT!! The integrity of selecting the Bible is actually twofold in this case. First, because I do, personally, believe the Bible, which translated, simply means the Book. Secondly, this 'Book' is the most documented accurate account of history in the world. With over 5,000 Greek manuscripts and more than 8,000 other manuscripts in Hebrew, Aramaic, and other languages of the times, it is the undisputed champion of consistently accurate history. You may question whether it is God's Word or not; that is, whether it is divinely inspired; but must accept the validity of the historical accounts and accuracy that it has to offer.

Personally, I admit proudly, yet with all humility and lacking of worthiness, that I do believe that it is God's Word, divinely inspired and written for our benefit so that we can learn from the Book's contents what we need to do to please our Creator and be adopted by Him; to live with Him. Nevertheless, the fact is that this Book, the Bible, holds incredible esteem and integrity as a foundation for this book you are now reading. So, if nothing else, take the Bible for what it is… the most read book, the best-seller of all books for centuries, a credible and dependable source of good commonsense healthy living concepts that can help you understand yourself much better; an Owner's Manual, of sorts.

If you are a Christian now, the concepts, ideas, and applications herein should help deepen your knowledge and awareness of, and indeed the very practice of your faith in your daily walk. You may laugh, you may cry, or you may just have a few of those proverbial reminding "Duh!" moments. Learning is all a matter of perspective. It's determined by the past experiences, current frame of mind, state of heart, level of faith, and compassionate passion of the learner. If any one of these is out of balance, learning will be skewed by the particular slanted interpretation of any given passage. Therefore, each of you will gain something different from this book, and probably something different each time you read it. So use this book as a reference as you stumble through this life, re-reading sections that you remember may apply to your current needs. Above all, seek your final answers in the Bible. You will be amazed at the answers you will find!

Everything shared is from strictly a biblical perspective and with scriptural support. No interjections of faith or belief from any man-made creeds are provided for guidance, but only for consideration and introspection as they may or may

In Pursuit…
not apply to you in encouraging you to challenge all
that you know and as you develop that precious gift of
independent thinking that we have each been given
and so seldom practice. The dynamics of this book
should help you to develop a mode of variable free-
thinking that will enable you to put into ready practice
those Christ-like traits as you approach the complex
situations that we all encounter everyday as Christians
in a non-Christian world.

Now, many of you reading this book that don't
believe in God or don't know the Gospel may be
asking yourself why you should continue reading, or
why you are even wasting your time. Let me assure
you, this is NOT wasting your time. Even if you have
no desire to learn about God, or have completely
closed your mind to the Bible, I believe that this
information will benefit you greatly in all aspects of
your life, because we answer some common
intriguing questions that are usually an interest to us
all. I also hope that this book will give you the insight
to something that you never knew existed, that peace
and comfort that every human seeks, and so few ever
truly find.

2 – The "Earthly Reason"

You may be asking yourself right now, "*What earthly reason would I have for wanting to devote that much time and energy into something that I've already heard about a thousand times over?!*" Well, let me tell you the "earthly reason".

Alright, now consider this from an even more practical perspective. The Bible only teaches you things that you know to be the healthiest, the least stressful, and that are unquestionably the right ways to live and maintain your health, integrity, and honor, so if for no other reasons than these, wouldn't you want to learn what it says and live that way anyway? If your car owner's manual says to put 10W/40 oil into your engine, are you going to put 90W oil in? Of course not! If a road sign shows you a 180 degree hairpin turn ahead, will you maintain your current speed or slow down? Well, slow down, of course! It's just that most uncommon of traits, Common Sense! So if the Bible tells you to avoid or do certain things, why won't you heed to that message? It was inspired by your Manufacturer, the one who made you. Wouldn't He have the best idea of how to maintain you as well? Even from a historical viewpoint, wouldn't you want to learn what people a few thousand years ago figured out was or wasn't healthy living, just simply from a historical and experienced perspective? It makes perfect sense to study this renowned book. The Bible has life lessons in it that can make even our grandfathers stories pale by comparison.

In our "hi-tech" culture, we all too often begin thinking how great we are and how gloriously intelligent we have become since Grandpa's days. Our technology seemingly promises to fix all of our problems and make all of our lives more comfortable, convenient, and stress-free. Yet the overwhelming evidence proves to us exactly the opposite. Never in the history of mankind has there been more stress; stress-related crimes, stress-related illnesses, stressed marriages and homes, stressed children at ever-increasing younger ages, and stress-related suicides. The numbers are absolutely devastating to comprehend! Look around, research some statistics on your own and you will see exactly what I mean.

For example, current statistics show that suicide is the third leading cause of death among youths aged 15-24. Young people attempt suicide at an alarmingly high rate: among 15-24 year olds, there is one suicide for every 100-200 attempts, which means that literally thousands of youths are screaming out for some help, some attention, some real life answers. Suicide is the sixth leading cause of death among youths aged 5-14. A youth suicide (aged 15-24) occurs every 100 minutes. Read some statistics gathered by the American Foundation for Suicide Prevention (AFSP):

National Statistics

General

- Over 34,000 people in the United States die by suicide every year.
- In 2007 (latest available data), there were 34,598 reported suicide deaths.
- Suicide is the fourth leading cause of death for adults between the ages of 18 and 65 years in the United States (28,628 suicides).
- Currently, suicide is the 11th leading cause of death in the United States.
- A person dies by suicide about every 15 minutes in the United States. An attempt is estimated to be made **once every minute**.
- Ninety percent of all people who die by suicide have a diagnosable psychiatric disorder at the time of their death, (which can include severe depression).
- There are four male suicides for every female suicide, but three times as many females as males attempt suicide.
- Every day, approximately 90 Americans take their own life, and 2,300 more attempt to do so.

In Pursuit…
Youth

- Suicide is the fifth leading cause of death among those 5-14 years old.
- Suicide is the third leading cause of death among those 15-24 years old.
- Between the mid-1950s and the late 1970s, the suicide rate among U.S. males aged 15-24 **more than tripled** (from 6.3 per 100,000 in 1955 to 21.3 in 1977). Among females aged 15-24, the rate **more than doubled** during this period (from 2.0 to 5.2).
- Among young people aged 10-14 years, the **rate has doubled in the last two decades**.
- Between 1980-1996, the suicide rate for African-American males aged 15-19 has also **doubled**.
- Risk factors for suicide among the young include suicidal thoughts, psychiatric disorders (such as depression, impulsive aggressive behavior, bipolar disorder, certain anxiety disorders), drug and/or alcohol abuse and previous suicide attempts, with the risk increased if there is situational stress and access to firearms.

Older People

- The suicide rates for men rise with age, most significantly after age 65.

- The rate of suicide in men 65+ is seven times that of females who are 65+.
- The suicide rates for women peak between the ages of 45-54 years old, and again after age 75.
- About 60 percent of elderly patients who take their own lives see their primary care physician within a few months of their death.
- Six to 9 percent of older Americans who are in a primary care setting suffer from major depression.
- More than 30 percent of patients suffering from major depression report suicidal ideation.
- Risk factors for suicide among the elderly include: a previous attempt, the presence of a mental illness, the presence of a physical illness, social isolation (some studies have shown this is especially so in older males who are recently widowed) and access to means, such as the availability of firearms in the home.

Depression and suicide are affecting all age groups across all ethnic and economic boundaries, and are on the increase. Young people can become emotionally distraught rather easily and thus are especially vulnerable to suicidal thoughts. Even knowing this, and knowing the statistical evidences, if you look at the movies, music, television programming, internet, and games that we and our children are completely immersed in 16-20 hours everyday, there is extreme violence, sexual promiscuity, and wickedness of every sort being force fed into their brains and written on their hearts. Yet we have the very mistaken idea and denial of the problem to just sit idly by believing that 4-5 hours per

In Pursuit…
week of "church" will repair all of this continual damage.

Would you pour orange juice into a glass and expect to taste milk when you drink it? Of course not! Would you pour water into the gas tank of your vehicle and expect it to run? Again, of course not. Then why do we think for even an instant that we can pour filth, misery, violence, sex, and evil into our minds or that of our children and expect anything pure and good to come out? It's absurd. We, too, are vessels. What is put in is the only thing that can come out.

What we seek in our society most often is not the truth, but justification. You seek to justify your lifestyle, your actions, and your thoughts. You don't want to hear anything that might contradict your life, but only those things that support it. Most of us, including you, usually become very offended, angry, and sometimes very vocal if we hear, see or read anything that speaks against or even questions our life or actions. Everything in our society has become prioritized for convenience, including our beliefs. It all has to feel good and comfortable and give us that "warm fuzzy" that we are wanting. Somehow we have the false belief that we possess all wisdom and knowledge about right or wrong based on our life experiences and teachings, that we have somehow ascertained the whole truth, therefore anything that challenges that thought pattern upsets us. Now, granted, there are some folks who know and admit that their current lifestyles are not right. They do become angry at these challenging principles, but their anger is more at themselves because they realize that they are not living right and simply are not willing to change, so they just don't want to hear the truth because it hurts. Knowing the truth and Living the truth are two very different things.

In Pursuit…
3 – Absolute Truth? or Absolute Truth!

While we are on the subject of truth and our society, I must address the idea of 'Absolute Truth' and whether it is a myth or a reality. In a plethora of surveys conducted by Christian and non-Christian groups, the results have been overwhelmingly the same with well over 80% of Americans believing that there is no "Absolute Truth' that we can all embrace as a nation as a common belief foundation.

Most replies were that what each individual believes to be 'right' or 'wrong' is the truth for them individually, but that those beliefs of 'right' or 'wrong' are different for each person, therefore rendering any common belief system unattainable for the nation or world as a whole. Most people in these studies did not believe that there is any "Absolute Truth", that there is no common moral absolute that exists. Most of these surveyed also concluded that we must respect ALL forms of religion, belief systems, and values, which to this writer is an impossibility and fallacy in and of itself. Let me explain.

If we buy into this "respect all" theory, then we must accept every thought pattern in the world, including; satanic religions, sexual preferences (which can include such atrocities as pedophiles, abusers, etc.), drug use, gangs, and many other forms of behavior that people would distort as a belief or value. If we state respect for 'all', then we are open to *anything* that someone can claim is *something* to them. Yet, those stating the "respect all" theory would emphatically disagree and say that we should only accept some certain behaviors or beliefs, because after all, some of those I stated are ludicrous, even illegal, right! Well, by whose 'beliefs and values' are we to choose only the acceptance of certain ones? By whose 'value system' are the laws based? You see, the "respect all" theory falls short and negates itself through the application of the core principle that it is based upon.

There are inherent issues in the mindset of "respect all". If that is true, that each individual develops their own set of beliefs of what is 'right' or what is 'wrong', then how do we then establish laws that apply to the masses? One of our constitutional rights is freedom of religion, or freedom of belief systems. If, then, a pedophile has a belief system that allows him to act upon his desires with clear conscience; or an abused woman reaches her physical and mental limits fearing herself and/or her children to be in danger and her beliefs clearly lead her to thinking murdering her abusive husband is the 'right' thing to do; are they truly criminal acts, or just acts of faith in their individual belief systems that is truth to them individually, which is their constitutional right to exercise as they see fit? There has to be a moral absolute for laws to even be presented, considered and passed.

You see, if you open up to the thought that there is no 'Absolute Truth' that we can all rely on as a common guide and basis to our thoughts and resulting actions, then there is little more than semi-controlled chaos. That is where juries get hung, where courts get confused even when the facts and evidence are clear, when we see unnatural acts being accepted in the streets and people being charged with hate crimes for stating their beliefs against those acts. An un-unified system of differing beliefs without a common agreed standard is what has caused wars in Middle East since before Jesus time; what has caused nations to war against themselves, whether Vietnam or our own Civil War. Dissociated belief systems wreak havoc within a nation, and within the world. There MUST be an 'Absolute Truth' that we can all embrace and build our country's foundation upon for us to continue being a successful and prosperous nation.

That 'Absolute Truth', that moral absolute, does indeed exist, and our country was founded upon that Truth in its beginning. Our founding fathers had firm beliefs in the Bible and the Absolute Truth that it teaches. Upon that Absolute Truth, they created the Constitution and the Amendments. For that Absolute Truth they risk their very lives, the lives of their families, and many died to allow that Truth to prevail in establishing our great country. That Truth is what has always made our nation a Great Nation among all nations of the world. Why do you suppose they placed 'One Nation under God' in the pledge of allegiance? Why do you think that you see In God We Trust on every denomination of money we have in our country? Those statements came from a conviction and commitment to that 'Absolute Truth'! It does exist, and it is right in front of every one of us in the form of a human instruction manual called the Bible, which simply means 'The Book'. It gives us 'Absolute Truth' without any excuses or extra fluff. We can deny it. We can ignore it. We can defy it. We can hate it. We can twist it. However, we cannot change it. It is the Truth, regardless of whether we like it or not, and regardless of whether we embrace it or not. The Book is the Absolute Truth that we all seek, if only we will look, listen, and heed.

With our country's current direction fast erupting into a combined civil religious internal battle

In Pursuit…

of national origin and personal rights, I find myself being called into more aggressive action... and I truly believe that there are many other typically conservative Christians that are hearing the same call because of our conviction and commitment to that Absolute Truth. Let me explain, again.

First, I am very thankful for the freedoms that we have in America, and fully realize the great blessings that we have and the strengths that are available for us to use in preserving our great nation. However, the religious rights that we were founded on now being perceived as unpopular among the many "special interest" groups concerns me greatly.

Somehow, the overwhelming majority of our American Christian community has opted for many decades now to remain silent, mumbling our disgust at many events and legislatures, but doing little to nothing to protect our position. I realize that there are many truly committed and active Christians, but sadly, as statistics attest to, these are the minority even among the Christian community as a whole.

Just as Christ was angered and felt it necessary to overturn the tables in the temple in order to protect

His Father's honor and place, it is proper time for us to exercise that same validated anger and start becoming more active in "overturning the tables" in our country.

Jesus told us that if we proclaim the Father before men that He will proclaim us before the Father, and if we do NOT proclaim the Father, neither will He proclaim us before Him. Our silent disapproval is not proclaiming our Father before men, and is in fact, expediting the agenda of the ungodly groups. Ours is truly a "silence of the lambs", being every bit as destructive to God as Hannibal was to those around him in the movie I am referring to.

We grumble and mumble, but these other groups boldly proclaim their allegiance to the wickedness and practices of man's desires as loudly as they can. We sign petitions and send emails, but these other groups rise up and attack mercilessly, violently attacking every belief in God and those that claim Him as they rage forward with their agendas. They march, parade, have annual events, approach school-age children, and even disrupt Christian gatherings and events in disorderly and threatening ways to intimidate us, the perceived "enemy." **While we need to first pray for them**, and I do NOT support the rising up of Christians in a full blown physical religious war, I DO question whether

In Pursuit…
Christians *as a whole* in our country understand who we are and Who we serve!

Let me warn you now, this next section will be uncomfortable! Yet all of this is spoken in Love. There are some basic ideas and concepts that I want to clarify right now, as we begin this discussion.

The purpose of this is best defined in **Colossians 2: 2 & 3** – "**[2]My purpose is that they may be encouraged in heart and united in love, so that they may have the full riches of complete understanding, in order that they may know the mystery of God, namely, Christ, [3]in whom are hidden all the treasures of wisdom and knowledge."**

#1 – This entire section is meant, in the purest of Love and Truth, to reach, teach, and preach straight from scriptural principles and Biblical Truth. No manmade interjections of creeds, doctrines, or rules… Only the Bible as the guide.

#2 – What I am presenting is sometimes hard to hear. There won't be any stepping on of toes, but most certainly WILL be mashing of feet , including mine, in an attempt to AVOID gnashing of teeth in the eternity.

#3 – When terms such as 'Warrior' and 'Battle' are used, the reference is to **our Spiritual arsenal of weapons – Intercessory Prayer; Proclaiming the Gospel; Honesty, to ourselves and to the world; and Sacrificial Love, even when it is a painful and tough love.**

When I speak of becoming more involved in 'the fight', this is NOT a cry to in ANY way attack the homosexual community, drug community, makers or users of pornography, nor any other group involved in sinful behavior.

This is Not a call to a Christian jihad, but a call to Christian Action. A holy war, but a Spiritual Holy war that ensued the moment that Adam fell into sin, and we have become far too passive about how we fight, or even if we fight.

On the contrary, it is to completely envelope them in prayer, present the Gospel to them, even if they reject it, and to continue to love them as Christ does, in constant prayers that they might be reached before their judgment day.

IN NO WAY does this mean Accepting their sinful behavior or Tolerating it to be perceived as "normal" or "ok" and flaunted in our families faces. This does NOT mean judging nor condemning them, but only acknowledging the sin for what it is; sin that is unacceptable in God's eyes as stated clearly and unmistakably in the scriptures. The person, however,

In Pursuit…

we love, and hope to save their soul. The sin, scripture condemns and God judges.

So, the cry and call of Christ referred to is that of the Great Commission… Teach and Preach the Gospel to every living creature.

Mark 16:15 & 16 – "[15]He said to them, "Go into all the world and preach the good news to all creation. [16]Whoever believes and is baptized will be saved, but whoever does not believe will be condemned."

That does not mean that all of those we teach will accept it, but our command is Not to Force-feed it and Demand that they accept, it is to offer the Truth of the Gospel in Love to them, even if they coldly reject it. Our call is only to Spread the seed, not reign over it.

Our duty as God's children is to gird the armor of Truth and rise up against the enemy. Our enemy is not the 'infidel', but the real enemy… Satan. We are out to destroy him and his power over us, as humans, by swinging the Sword of Truth in every direction around us.

Ephesians 6:10-18 talks about The Armor of God

"[10]Finally, be strong in the Lord and in his mighty power. [11]Put on the full armor of God so that you can take your stand against the devil's schemes. [12]For our struggle is not against flesh and blood, but against the rulers, against the authorities, against the powers of this dark world and against the spiritual forces of evil in the heavenly realms. [13]Therefore put on the full armor of God, so that when the day of evil comes, you may be able to stand your ground, and after you have done everything, to stand. [14]Stand firm then, with the belt of truth buckled around your waist, with the breastplate of righteousness in place, [15]and with your feet fitted with the readiness that comes from the gospel of peace. [16]In addition to all this, take up the shield of faith, with which you can extinguish all the flaming arrows of the evil one. [17]Take the helmet of salvation and the sword of the Spirit, which is the word of God. [18]And pray in the Spirit on all occasions with all kinds of prayers and requests. With this in mind, be alert and always keep on praying for all the saints."

Do we fully understand the strength of Him whom we serve? Do we understand that our Leader is the One who raised men from the dead? Who healed with a simple touch, or with words spoken from His lips? Do we remember that our Leader parted an entire sea and dried the ground beneath it to deliver His people? That He alone spoke our very being and our entire completely perfect ordered universe into existence? Do we remember that it was OUR Father that even Satan had to consult with and get permission from to test Job, and that afterwards God rewarded Job with far MORE than he had before he was tested?

Why do we appear weak, intimidated and afraid? Why does the world intimidate us, or do man's laws and the threat of jail scare us so? The apostles knew persecution far beyond what we will ever experience in this country. They were stoned, beheaded, and publicly shamed prior to their violent deaths... just for proclaiming their Father, our Father, before men. Are some of us so weak and filled with doubt in our Father's abilities that we would rather stay silent and let His honor and place be mocked and made into a political marketplace? That we may be found guilty of not sharing His Word and Gospel because we are not comfortable?

Although I do NOT support a religious war in our country, I do state very clearly, based upon the Word of God, that we ARE and always have been involved in a spiritual war, and that we ARE here to openly and boldly proclaim our Father and His Word, and that if we do NOT do so NOW, that we are in dire jeopardy of having Jesus, our Christ & Savior, not proclaiming our name before the Father. If we aren't sharing His Word, or speaking out because we fear being questioned in ways that we do not know how to respond, then you better blow the dust off of that Bible and start studying "to present yourself approved." If you are one of the Christian soldiers involved in the fight, then I commend you.

2 Timothy 2:15 (New King James Version)
[15] Be diligent to present yourself approved to God, a worker who does not need to be ashamed, rightly dividing the word of truth.

2 Timothy 3:16-18 (New King James Version)
[16] All Scripture *is* given by inspiration of God, and *is* profitable for doctrine, for reproof, for correction, for instruction in righteousness, [17] that the man of God may be complete, thoroughly equipped for every good work.

2 Timothy 4:2 (New King James Version)
[2] Preach the word! Be ready in season *and* out of season. Convince, rebuke, exhort, with all longsuffering and teaching.

In Pursuit…

Make this a little more personal, and make no mistakes... God loves you, but he did destroy Sodom and countless others that denied Him. In your silence, we you denying Him. With that being said, are you also living just as Sodomites? Aren't you denying Him as you silently let His name, His honor, and His place that established our country be overtaken by political marketers that act as puppets and are promoting "special interest" group agendas at frightening rates?

Leviticus 26:30-33 (New King James Version)
[30] I will destroy your high places, cut down your incense altars, and cast your carcasses on the lifeless forms of your idols;
and My soul shall abhor you.
[31] I will lay your cities waste and bring your sanctuaries to desolation, and I will not smell the fragrance of your sweet aromas.
[32] I will bring the land to desolation, and your enemies who dwell in it shall be astonished at it.
[33] I will scatter you among the nations and draw out a sword after you;
your land shall be desolate and your cities waste.

As American Christians, with more human and financial resources than any other country on this planet, are we not responsible for not only our country, but for setting the example and precedence of Christianity and Christian rights the world over? If we cannot proclaim God's Word before our own openly and confident in His ability to change our own people, than how can we profess to send out missionaries with full confidence that our Father can also change those that we proclaim Him to in other countries? I realize that we spread the Seed where the ground is most fertile, but is it you or I that have the right to determine who is worthy to hear the Word, what is or is not fertile ground? The scripture didn't say "go preach the Gospel to every living creature that you decide is ready to hear"! The scripture just says "go preach the Word to every living creature". We plant, but only God gives the growth.

Either we have confidence and faith in our Leader, our Father, or we don't. We cannot honestly claim that peace through Him anywhere if we lack the strength, or the conviction, or the hope and trust in Him to change our own country in His sovereign plan for us. We cannot call on Him only in times of trouble and despair, whether as individuals or a country as a whole, and expect any positive response. Our God is a fair and just God, but expects us to obey Him and His commands, to have an honest change of heart, for us to be heard.

In Pursuit…

Our defense is to convert to offense. Our offense is only offending to Satan and his followers, which is exactly where we need to be... addressing those who are lost. Our defense is to boldly begin proclaiming our God, our Father, our Hope, our Faith, and His Word WITHOUT fear of consequence. If He is our focus, then nothing stops us or slows us in accomplishing what He has instructed us to do... "Preach the Gospel to EVERY living creature," and that includes those here that are pressing Satan's agenda so adamantly. Jesus stated that He came to seek and save the lost. We have a critical mission in our own country right now to do the very same thing, and *the beauty of this* is that the lost are now coming to us, confronting us. What a wonderful time to start sharing His Absolute Truth with them.

If we were in a physical war with a physical General giving us direct orders, many of us would be dishonorably discharged or thrown into the brig for disobeying direct orders. So why in this world or in heaven would we ever think that our Commander and Christ would proclaim us before the General, our God, when we are not fighting for Him as He gave us such direct orders to do?! Stand up, fellow Christian! Arise, prepare yourself for battle! Arm yourself with the Word and a thorough knowledge of it! Fire back at the enemy, use the Sword of Truth and boldly march into this battle with the assurance that the Commanders of these opposing forces have already met and you KNOW WITHOUT A DOUBT that YOU ARE ALREADY VICTORIOUS!

The ONLY way that you can lose is if you become a traitor and begin fighting for the other side. You have already won! *We do not fear in the dark what is true in the Light!* If you see clearly what is there in the Light, those things do not change just because it has become dark. So what is stopping us from boldly and loudly marching into this fight? Why are we so scared? Why are we mumbling? We need to quit looking back and join the front! God's plan WILL succeed, because He always finds those He needs to lead His cause. The question is; are you listening to Him? Are YOU going to be the one that goes with Him, because He is asking?

We need only to look at God's Word to discover His plan and His Truth for us. Neither the creeds of man, nor additional man-made instructions are needed, but only His Word that has been inspired and delivered to us. The call is clear.

In Pursuit…
4 – Who Are You, As The Reader?

Before you go any further in reading this book, I think it is only fair that you honestly discover who you are first. Where are you in your life and beliefs from a spiritual perspective? Now, this applies to you, whether you claim the name of Christian, as well as you who may consider yourself a firm atheist, agnostic, or other form of belief. You need to understand exactly who and where you are now so that you can safe-guard against any of those prejudices or pre-determined automatic responses that accompany your current beliefs, as the whole point of this book is to get you to think for yourself, not as any label, stereotype, or according to any man-written creed. Also, in order to determine where you are going, you need to know where you are now. We all have the same Word and the same destination, but we may each need to take certain specific steps in our own lives to get us to that path from where we are today. You may think that the answer is very clear to you now, but let me present some thoughts and have you re-think your current position.

Let's start with some basic definitions from Dictionary.com as a basis for this conversation. Most people around the world define a believer in much the same way, as one who believes in one true God, believes that Jesus was His son, and that the Bible is divinely inspired; a person following the basic biblical beliefs. But I want to define four distinct common types of nonbeliever, because I think that is where we may run into some confusion if we don't define those the same from the onset.

The ATHEIST, AGNOSTIC, INFIDEL, & SKEPTIC refer to persons not inclined toward belief in God or a particular form of Biblical belief. An ATHEIST is one who denies the existence of a deity or of divine beings. This person just outright believes that they KNOW that God does not exist. An AGNOSTIC is one who believes it impossible to know anything about God or about the creation of the universe and refrains from commitment to any religious doctrine. Basically, the agnostic is unsure; they just don't know. INFIDEL means an unbeliever, especially a nonbeliever in Islam or, in some cases, Christianity. The infidel is generally regarded as an unbeliever in the broadest sense, meaning that the infidel is an unbeliever for any number of reasons or by any number of definitions. The infidel has heard the Truth, but plainly denies it as Truth. A SKEPTIC doubts and is

In Pursuit...
critical of all accepted doctrines and creeds, generally whether God-made or man-made.

Let me first say that I don't believe that any true atheists exist, nor that it is even possible for them to exist, and definitely that I do not have enough 'faith' to be an atheist! That may sound ludicrous now, but let me explain. I say that with the premise that the definition of an atheist is a person who denies what they believe to KNOW, that God doesn't exist. Let me ask you this, if you claim to be atheist, do you know even one half of everything that there is to know in the universe? No one can honestly answer that with a 'Yes'. So, now let me ask you this, if you don't know at least one half of everything that there is to know, isn't it possible that somewhere in that other half there may be something that could prove to you that there is, in fact, a God? The reply is generally something along the lines of, "Well, I guess it's possible, although not likely, and it would take some amazing proof for me to believe that it's even possible." (A little sidebar here... it always amazes me, in a humorous way, to think that these people that completely deny the existence of God will create company policies and buy special insurance policies that mention "acts of God"!) Yet, on a serious note, they cannot honestly deny the existence of anything based on complete knowledge, as no one person possesses all knowledge of all things. Therefore, if they deny the existence of God, it is based upon limited knowledge, past and present education levels on the subject, and is swayed greatly by past and present experiences combined with peer influence and a disinterest in learning more. That's not a negative 'hit' against those who claim the name of atheist, just an observation. The key factor, of course, is that person's lack of interest in pursuing more knowledge on the subject. And most atheists are devout believers in evolution, which is another long discussion entirely. Yet, to believe in evolution takes an incredible amount of blind faith in denying all scientific facts and principles of simple physics. Not going to go into tremendous detail now, but you'll understand a little more, later in this book, in A Sampling Review of Man's Theories, where you can scratch the surface of the details that I am eluding to here.

According to the questions and typical responses discussed above, I believe that those who proclaim to be atheist usually fall more into a combination of agnostic skeptics. This is a good thing, however. Agnostics and skeptics simply mean that they are doubters. It doesn't matter how much of a doubter as much as it matters, what kind. There are

In Pursuit…
two basic types of doubters, the honest doubter and the dishonest doubter.

The honest doubter is the person who isn't sure whether God exists or not; who isn't sure whether Jesus was the Son of God or not; who isn't sure whether the Bible is really God's Word or not, but wants to know. They want to learn and research for themselves, then make up their mind after discovering all there is to discover about it, when they can make an intelligent decision. This person can claim to be an atheist, an agnostic, a skeptic, or sadly, even claim to be a Christian. We have honest doubters in the church today. We have people attending worship services every time the doors are open, and active in every aspect of church work and ministry today that STILL are walking around with hearts full of doubt, yet they are there because they want to know more. Let me say, though, that we also have people with absolutely not one lingering shadow of a doubt as to Who they belong to or Whose they are. They are as sure of there being a God and a Son and His Word being the divine writings that they are, as they are that they must breathe air to live.

The dishonest doubter… this is the person who isn't sure whether God exists or not; who isn't sure whether Jesus was the Son of God or not; who isn't sure whether the Bible is really God's Word or not, just like the honest doubter, except has absolutely no interest in knowing. Notice the difference here? The honest doubter and the dishonest doubter only have one differentiating trait. The honest doubter wants to know. The dishonest doubter has no interest at all in knowing. He believes that he has this world, universe, and everything in it all figured out, and he just doesn't want to waste his time with any of this perceived foolery. The dishonest doubter is the person who would generally be referred to in some circles as the infidel. What makes this person dishonest is found in the first of the Four Factors of Light that we will discuss in a later chapter. However, I do not think that any dishonest doubters would have wandered in to pick this book up and learn anything more, so you are probably going to enjoy continuing on.

5 – Is God Fact or Fiction?

So, does God exist or not? Does it even matter? Using our standard cultural labels, it seems we're all becoming materialists, naturalists, relativists, humanists, hedonists, or other culturally-honed "bots" that seem to think we have it pretty well together. Many believe that metaphysical thought is for philosophers and theologians; that "religion" is OK for those who need a crutch to limp on through a difficult life, and that anyone who does believe in God or attends church is just another one of the brain-washed masses. Nothing could be more opposite of the real truth. Philosophical truth is actually right below the surface, and this book should enlighten you to at least some of that truth.

You see, living without God, without any hope of something better than this world and its troubles, is kind of like living in the desert with a mirage as your water source. You can go to it every day to quench your insatiable thirst, but each time you dig deeper, you still end up with a bucket of hot dry sand. And if, by chance, you happen across a small amount of moisture in the sand, after sucking out the moisture, you still have the dry grit of sand in your mouth, and you always want more. There is no refreshing using worldly things as your source of joy. There is no quenching the human desire by earthly means or treasures of this world. If you are at the top of your game, you still desire more. It never stops!

What we're talking about here is something that WILL quench that thirst. The desire for more is always present, as that is in our nature as physical beings, but it is not in our spiritual nature to crave worldly things. In our spiritual nature, we were made to worship, and worship we do. Think carefully about this. Either we worship God, or some other form of spirituality, or we worship money or some other material form.

Merriam-Webster Dictionary online contains the following definition of '**worship**';
Etymology: Middle English worshipe worthiness, respect, reverence paid to a divine being, from Old English weorthscipe worthiness, respect, from weorth worthy, worth + -scipe -ship
Date: before 12th century
1chiefly British : a person of importance —used as a title for various officials (as magistrates and some mayors)
2: reverence offered a divine being or supernatural power ; also : an act of expressing such reverence

In Pursuit...

3: a form of religious practice with its creed and ritual

4: extravagant respect or admiration for or devotion to an object of esteem <worship of the dollar>

Now, look at these descriptions. Isn't it interesting that even our most common definitions includes what we see in number 4, worship of the dollar? Number 1 is primarily used to address certain high ranking officials in the British government, but all other definitions refer to actions. 'Reverence offered', 'an act of expressing such reverence', 'religious practice', 'respect to'; all of these refer to some form of action. Even the terms 'admiration' and 'devotion' tell us action is involved. If you greatly admire or are devoted to something, then you act upon those feelings to either be close to it or obtain more of it. Worship is not just a 'Bible term'.

Also notice the definitions that Merriam-Webster gives us for '**Religious**';

- *elating to or manifesting faithful devotion to an acknowledged ultimate reality or deity*

- *crupulously and conscientiously faithful*

Religious is an adjective describing a form of action. According to Webster's definition, the word Religious is also not just a 'Bible term'. In fact, the word Religious is not necessarily a positive term. Simply looking at these two words, we can ascertain that all of us are religious and worship something. Maybe it's God, maybe an earthly person, or it could be money, a hobby, a sport, or anything that you have *conscientiously* attached yourself to in a devoted and faithful fashion. The point here is simple… whether you believe in God and what the Bible teaches or not, you are made to worship, and you do, religiously to something, whether to an acknowledged reality or deity.

God is the only acknowledged reality <u>and</u> deity. To believe anything different negates the very foundations of faith in anything, and demonstrates an undeniable arrogance in that we deny the existence of a divine Creator. Such arrogance by man is exactly why Satan has such power over us here.

So, does God exist or not? Does it even matter? Keep reading and see what makes sense to you.

6 - A Sampling Review of Man's Theories

Ok, this is going to be a long and controversial section, **but stay with me now**. This should at least open your mind somewhat. Since the beginning of time, which by the way, has only been about 6,000 years, not billions… alright, getting ahead of myself (we'll talk about this in another chapter)… since the beginning of time, men have been trying to figure out and explain how we and this earth came to be in existence. Now, let me say right here and now, **my** family tree doesn't have any monkeys or single cell relatives in it as far as I know, although we all act or think like that at times. However, I will try to keep an open mind and perspective as we review some of man's ideas, theories and concepts about where we came from, how we should live, and where we should seek happiness, and will only present facts, not opinions.

Please keep in mind throughout this Chapter that the primary purpose is to start you studying and learning more on your own. It is NOT my intent here to review <u>every</u> manmade theory available, nor to dive in to great depths about these that are presented. This is all just scratching the surface and presenting but a few points in each. Again, the intent is to make you think and inspire you to dig deeper on your own if that is your desire.

Theories

Ok, let's define some of these theories first. We'll start with Darwin, since that seems to be the most well known evolutionary theory that we hear about, and most seem to fall back on his theories at some point anyway.

Darwin's Theory of Evolution - The Premise

Darwin's Theory of Evolution is the widely held notion that all life is related and has descended from a common ancestor: the birds and the bananas, the fishes and the flowers -- all related. Darwin's general theory presumes the development of life from non-life and stresses a purely naturalistic (undirected) "descent with modification". That is, complex creatures evolve from more simplistic ancestors naturally over time. In a nutshell, as random genetic mutations occur within an organism's genetic code, the beneficial mutations are preserved because they aid survival -- a process known as "natural selection." These beneficial mutations are passed on to the next generation. Over time, beneficial mutations accumulate and the result is

In Pursuit…

an entirely different organism (not just a variation of the original, but an entirely different creature or species). So, in layman's terms, if an organism makes a change that is good, that helps it survive better, then it keeps that good change and passes it on.

Darwin's Theory of Evolution - Natural Selection

Interesting fact to start with: About 150 years ago, Darwin was a young amateur scientist who boarded a ship headed out to explore the world. His personal quest was to determine how the world works and what made it like it is. His Theory of Evolution was born from his writings about his journey and the things that he had seen.

While Darwin's Theory of Evolution is a relatively young archetype, the evolutionary worldview itself is as old as antiquity. Ancient Greek philosophers such as Anaximander postulated the development of life from non-life and the evolutionary descent of man from animal. Charles Darwin simply brought something new to the old philosophy -- a plausible mechanism called "natural selection." Natural selection acts to preserve and accumulate minor advantageous genetic mutations. Suppose a member of a species developed a functional advantage (it grew wings and learned to fly). Its offspring would inherit that advantage and pass it on to their offspring. The inferior (disadvantaged) members of the same species would gradually die out, leaving only the superior (advantaged) members of the species. Natural selection is the preservation of a functional advantage that enables a species to compete better in the wild.

Darwin's Theory of Evolution - Slowly But Surely...

Darwin's Theory of Evolution is a slow gradual process. Darwin wrote, *"…Natural selection acts only by taking advantage of slight successive variations; she can never take a great and sudden leap, but must advance by short and sure, though slow steps."*

Thus, Darwin conceded that, *"If it could be demonstrated that any complex organ existed, which could not possibly have been formed by numerous, successive, slight modifications, my theory would absolutely break down."* Such a complex organ would be known as an "irreducibly complex system". An irreducibly complex system is one composed of multiple parts, all of which are necessary for the system to function. If even one part is missing, the entire system will fail to function. Every individual part is integral. Thus, such a system could not have evolved slowly, piece by piece.

Darwin's Theory of Evolution - A Theory in Crisis

Darwin's Theory of Evolution is a theory in crisis in light of the tremendous advances we've made in molecular biology, biochemistry and genetics over the past fifty years. We now know that there are in fact tens of thousands of irreducibly complex systems on the cellular level. Specified complexity pervades the microscopic biological world.

Molecular biologist Michael Denton wrote, *"Although the tiniest bacterial cells are incredibly small, weighing less than 10^{-12} grams, each is in effect a veritable micro-miniaturized factory containing thousands of exquisitely designed pieces of intricate molecular machinery, made up altogether of one hundred thousand million atoms, far more complicated than any machinery built by man and absolutely without parallel in the non-living world."*

And we don't need a microscope to observe irreducible complexity. The eye, the ear and the heart are all examples of irreducible complexity, though they were not recognized as such in Darwin's day. Nevertheless, Darwin confessed, *"To suppose that the eye with all its inimitable contrivances for adjusting the focus to different distances, for admitting different amounts of light, and for the correction of spherical and chromatic aberration, could have been formed by natural selection seems, I freely confess, absurd in the highest degree."*

With the scientific evidence that we now have proving some organs to be irreducibly complex, and even Darwin's own statements, how is it that so many learned people, especially doctorate-level men and women in the scientific community, how is it that they do not see the invalidation of the evolutionistic theories? The evidence is overwhelming. What I have presented here is a very, very small sampling of the evidence that exists.

Now, let's briefly acknowledge some other theories and belief systems, and then we'll revert back to a summarization of these to address the matter of origin regardless of belief.

In Pursuit…
Existentialism – (*From Wikipedia*)

Existentialism is a term that has been applied to the work of a group of nineteenth and twentieth century philosophers who, despite doctrinal differences, shared the belief that philosophical thinking begins with the human subject—not merely the thinking subject, but the acting, feeling, living human individual. In existentialism, the individual's starting point is characterized by what has been called "*the existential attitude*" or a sense of disorientation and confusion in the face of an apparently meaningless or absurd world.

The most famous of the Existentialist philosophers is the French author Jean-Paul Sartre.

Many existentialists have also regarded traditional systematic or academic philosophy, in both style and content, as too abstract and remote from concrete human experience. Like "rationalism" and "empiricism," "existentialism" is a term that belongs to intellectual history. Its definition is thus to some extent one of historical convenience. The term was explicitly adopted as a self-description by Jean-Paul Sartre, and through the wide dissemination of the postwar literary and philosophical output of Sartre and his associates.

Those most often associated with "existentialism" failed to form a cohesive philosophical discipline based on existential theories. Existentialism, while taught at universities, cannot point to leaders in the same way idealism or rationalism can. As you read the works of "existentialists" you come to see divisions and paradoxes not only between individuals, but within the works of many of the thinkers.

Dictionaries and first-year philosophy texts offer simple definitions of existentialism:

The doctrine that existence takes precedence over essence and holding that man is totally free and responsible for his acts.

This responsibility is the source of dread and anguish that encompass mankind. *- Webster's New World Dictionary, Second College Edition*; William Collins Publishers, Inc.; Cleveland, Ohio; 1979

A philosophy that emphasizes the uniqueness and isolation of the individual experience in a hostile or indifferent universe, regards human existence as unexplainable, and stresses freedom of choice and responsibility for the consequences of one's acts. -

In Pursuit…

Existentialism is largely a revolt against traditional European philosophy. Early existentialists tried to produce principles of knowledge that would be objective, universally true, and certain; yet they argue that objective, universal, and certain knowledge is an unattainable ideal. The existentialists reject the methods and ideals of science as being improper for philosophy.

Existentialism became influential in the mid-1900s. World War II (1939–1945) gave rise to widespread feelings of despair and of separation from the established order. These feelings led to the idea that people have to create their own values in a world in which traditional values no longer govern. Existentialism insists that choices have to be made arbitrarily by individuals, who thus create themselves, because there are no objective standards to determine choice.

To learn more about Existentialism, you may want to refer to an out-of-print text, *The New Dictionary of Existentialism*, by St. Elmo Nauman, Jr. If you can locate a copy, this lexicon provides an entire dictionary of specific words/terms as defined by the Existentialists. What is most interesting about Existentialism is that even these definitions become controversial among those who claim to be Existentialists; and Existentialism itself is as much literary as it is philosophical because of its strong influence from Sartre's writings. Whether it is a philosophy or a science is still very controversial as well.

UNIFORMITARIANISM – (*FROM WIKIPEDIA*)

Uniformitarianism has had two separate meanings, both more prevalent in 19th-century discourse:

- Within religious philosophy, Uniformitarianism ("with a capital U") is the belief that the Universe has existed as it is now for an infinite time and will continue to exist forever. This view is opposed to traditional theological views and modern science.

- Within scientific philosophy, uniformitarianism ("with a small u") refers to the principle that the same processes that shape the universe occurred in the past as they do now, and that the same laws of physics apply in all parts of the knowable universe. This is axiomatic. (*In traditional logic, an* **axiom** *or* **postulate** *is a proposition that is not proved or demonstrated but considered to be either self-evident, or subject to necessary decision.*) Therefore, its truth is taken for granted, and serves as a starting point for deducing and inferring other (theory dependent) truths. Principle, not often referred to as an "-ism" in modern discussions, is particularly relevant to geology and other sciences that operate on a long timescale such as astronomy and paleontology. The leading geologist of Charles Darwin's era, a Scot named Charles Lyell (1797 – 1875), incorporated James Hutton's gradualism into a theory known as uniformitarianism. The term refers to Lyell's idea that geological processes have not changed throughout Earth's history. Thus, for example, the forces that build mountains and erode mountains and the rates at which these forces operate are the same today as in the past.

CONFUCIANISM

Confucianism is basically a *humanistic social philosophy*. What this means can best be seen by contrasting *humanism* with *naturalism* and *supernaturalism.*

HUMANISM

Humanism: the philosophical belief that the welfare and happiness of mankind in this life is of primary concern. (In this century, the label has been used for *naturalistic humanists* who reject all religious beliefs, insisting that we should be *exclusively* concerned with human welfare in this, the *only* world.) Hence, people, rather than God or nature, are taken as ultimate. There is nothing superior to man as a source of human principles. **Consequent Spiritual Ideals**: The answer to the question, "How can goodness and happiness be achieved?" is gotten by pointing to the *principles of action found within man himself*--humaneness.

In Pursuit…
NATURALISM

Naturalism: the philosophical belief that what is studied by the social and physical sciences is all that exists (and the need for any explanation going beyond the universe is denied). Why cannot the Universe's existence and fundamental characteristics be themselves the ultimate features of explanation?
Consequential Spiritual Ideals: Hence, discovering how human beings should act is a matter of discovering how nature acts, so man's actions can be in accord with nature.

a. Trust instincts: by acting in accord with nature; what seems superhuman feats become possible.
b. By being in tune with nature, we become far more aware of the realm of possibilities.
c. We don't fight nature; we don't wish things were different; we don't force events to happen. (Instead of carrying the boat, the boat carries you.)
d. We become at one with the world--e.g., Zen and Taoism

SUPERNATURALISM

Supernaturalism: the theological belief that a force or power other than man or nature is ultimate.

a. This supernatural force (God) regulates both man and nature, making both of them subordinate to it. (God as creator.)
b. Man is considered to be higher than the rest of nature.

Consequent Spiritual Ideals: How human beings should act is largely a
matter of knowing and doing God's will. Hence, human beings must transcend themselves and not trust their instincts.

NIHILISM

Nihilism: A viewpoint that traditional values and beliefs are unfounded and that existence is senseless and useless; a doctrine that denies any objective ground of truth, and especially moral truths.

Nihilism is a doctrine or belief that conditions in the social organization are so bad as to make destruction desirable for its own sake, independent of any constructive program or possibility. It was the program of a 19th century Russian party advocating

In Pursuit…
revolutionary reform and using terrorism and
assassination as its primary tools of gain.

THEORIES SUMMARY

I believe this is enough review of some of the most
common theories being presented and practiced today.
Although there are many more, the purpose of this
book is not to present and teach about the theories, but
only to present them with their basic premises so that
we can address them with equal understanding. Ok,
we'll move on from here.

We will address these theories now only briefly
and from the single cell perspective initially, because
if we evolved from some form of primate or
Neanderthal, or subscribe to any of the theories
presented here, then there still had to be a beginning
for those as well, which would point us back to the
"Big Bang", resulting in the single cell theory
anyway, and so this seems a logical starting point that
will provide a high-level 30,000 foot review of the
others. Obviously, there are many, many other
theories that exist out there today, but I want to
address just these few here now. I believe that we can
make our point clearly and move on.

Evolution is a concept as old as the Greeks. Darwin's Theory was not new, but offered a new component to the already existing theory of evolution. The concept that Darwin offered to explain how and why evolution occurred was that of Natural Selection. This concept stated that through the course of time, a species, including a single cell, would develop new capabilities for survival. As it identified and mutated these changes into itself, the resulting offspring would have this new trait, causing the new species to live on with the 'improvements', while the old would eventually die off. This new offspring would also develop additional new traits, and so on.

The general nature and definition of evolution applies all the way back to the single cell theory, that we somehow through chance occurrences and the evolution of some single cell organisms that arose from the primordial seas, evolved over several million years into more and more complex creatures until we became what we are today. There are some basic problems with that theory however, especially when coupled with the Natural Selection addition that Darwin provided.

The initial obvious problem is that according to Darwin, the Natural Selection process meant that the evolution taking place were only traits needed for the new species to survive. We, as the complex creatures that we are today have more non-survival traits than survival traits. The ability to hunt, eat, stay sheltered from inclement weather, stay warm, or cool down as needed, procreate to assure our species lives on and survives, etc., those are survival traits. Yet we have the ability to love, reason, and discover things quite unnecessary for our survival. We can explore other galaxies, understand how complex a single cell actually is, and a thousand other non-survival traits. So, if evolution and Natural Selection are based upon the premise that each small, gradual change was to assure and increase the odds of survival, from where and why did we get these other very complex non-survival traits? And why would these other traits not have died off in previous 'versions' of humans, since they are non-survival traits?

Another discovery that has basically proven Darwin's theories obsolete is the discovery of thousands of "irreducibly complex systems" in the human body at the cellular level alone.

The next logically sequenced problem with this is where did these single cells come from to begin with? Even if you take it back to the 'Big Bang' theory that says the earth and planets, etc. all came from these random collisions of other planets, asteroids, or giant meteors, or even a mini-bang of single cells or atoms, then where did they come from? There is always that looming question that is never answered.

The scientific community overall has come to the ultimate conclusion that in order for the most basic and fundamental laws to exist as they do now in this exquisitely balanced, finely tuned universe, it all had to come into existence at the same time, which creates quite a dilemma for those scientists still trying to define our origin using the multiple theories available. These fundamental laws are things such as gravity, mass, speed of light, etc. If even one of the fundamental laws is changed, even slightly, or is eliminated or missing, then no life as we know it could exist. Therefore, it all had to come into existence simultaneously or nothing works. For all of the planets and fundamental laws to have simultaneously occurred by a random chance event is simply preposterous. However, there are still those who cling to the notion that it was just always there, which again creates quite a dilemma for these scientists. This in and of itself still defeats the ultimate goal of defining origin, because if it was already always there, then now we have new unanswerable questions. "Always there" denotes no beginning, and hence, no origin, so how have we answered the question of our origin if we somehow came into being from these random events of "always there/existing" masses of matter in space? Where did that space come from and how did those masses of matter form into planets and other objects? What in these events could have created life, even a single cell of life? And what about time? If these things were "always there", then there is no meaning or reality of the concept of time.

The only other option that these people are left with is that there was some type of design, intelligent design, to put these laws and fine-tuning together for some purpose, and maybe for the purpose of sustaining life as we know it. Yet, if that is an option, then many of the doctorate-level community will have to accept the fact that much of what they have been taught over numerous years of education and by peer-level groups is false. Now pride enters and raises its ugly head in arrogance to the only plausible explanation, jeering those who may consider such perceived nonsense to possibly have credence. It's a difficult situation to be in for them, yet a necessary one to reach the truth and begin to explore and teach the truth.

The next issue to consider, which is simply a fact, is the time of Darwin's life. In the 19th century, it was believed that cells were just this glob of simple protoplasmic material, a simple mass. In the 1950's and since, we have made tremendous advances in technology that have helped us discover that the simplest of single cells are very complex 'molecular machines'. Even 'simple' bacterial cells are not so simple, but extremely complex. Very similar to an outboard boat motor design, complete with a drive shaft, u-joint, & propeller, these 'simple cells' have very complex structure that incorporate solar power converted to useable energy and have 'trucks' that supply that energy throughout the cell when and where it is needed. They have extremely complex replication abilities that actually de-strand sections of DNA, decode it, copy it, transport it, and replicate it. The 'propeller' of these cells turns at about 100,000 RPM, yet can counter-rotate just ¼ of a turn and immediately 'stop on a dime' and redirect itself propelling at 100,000 RPM again instantly.

The more that is learned about these simplest of cells, the more scientists are assured that there has to have been a very distinct design, which means there had to be a Designer. No other clear explanations have been given as to these simple cellular functions and abilities or how they could have evolved using the Natural Selection theory.

In Pursuit…

The last issue we will address here is a remaining daunting fact, the existence of DNA, that complex string of proteins and amino acids in a specific genetic coded order. Natural Selection depends upon the idea that the cell was able to self-replicate. However, without DNA there is no self-replication; and without self-replication there is no natural selection. So, you cannot use natural selection to explain the origin of DNA without assuming the very existence of the thing that you're trying to explain. Therefore, the idea of intelligent design suddenly becomes more acceptable and plausible as you study the subject in depth. It is at this level of molecular genetics where we see the most compelling evidence of intelligent design. The study and understanding of the cellular function at the molecular level is amazing and humbling, and I would encourage every reader to visit the website **http://www.allaboutscience.org/darwins-theory-of-evolution.htm** and view the videos there. Some amazing and interesting information is there that may enlighten you.

The fact is, we could continue with this subject for another thousand pages, discussing the pitfalls of Existentialism, Uniformitarianism, and all of the other theories, and still not uncover all of the scientific evidence available to negate these concepts. The point is that the more we theorize and discover through complex analysis of anything in science, the more we are redirected back to the idea of a Master Designer at some juncture, whether it be God or some advanced alien species, but some form of intelligent design and Designer. Personally, I choose God, but that's your decision to make for yourself.

So, you might be saying or thinking, *"Yeah, so what?! Blah, blah, blah… you didn't prove or disprove anything to me here."* As I stated in the beginning of this chapter, the intent wasn't to prove or disprove anything, actually, but rather to perhaps enlighten your thinking a bit, to help you understand the complexities of our world a little better and understand what the definitions of some of the most common theories and beliefs are out there today. I just want to inspire you to THINK, explore, study, and understand where science is really leading us as we become better enabled to explore our universe, big and small. We are programmed all of our lives to simply listen, learn, believe what we are taught, and go perform according to those doctrines, whether right or wrong. I just want you to stop and think; question those things that you've learned and keep learning. Make intelligent decisions about your life; the 'now' and the hereafter.

7 – How Old Is Our Earth?

Now, I can talk more about what I started in Chapter 1. How old is our earth? How old can the planets be? How old can the other galaxies in our universe be? How long ago did the dinosaurs walk the earth, or did they at all? We all have questions that we don't understand, but hear about or see shows about on TV, so we listen to them and try to believe what they tell us because we certainly do not have the time, nor the expertise to chase down all of the answers for ourselves… or do we?

Now here is something to think about… IF there is a Master Designer out there, a God that was able to create all things, isn't it just possible that He may have made things already matured, aged, or old? Isn't it possible that He would also have the power to create things one way, then change how they work? Or maybe advance the timelines a bit by using certain physical and/or divine interventions? After all, according to Genesis, He created a man, then a woman… not a baby boy and a baby girl, right? And He made birds, not chicks; fish, not guppies; and trees, not planting seeds. It would only be logical to assume that with the maturity of all of these other things that He also made other geological formations in a mature state as well. Maybe it takes gazillions (my own word) of years for our world to make coal, or oil, or diamonds, etc., but if a Creator could breathe the stars into existence and form the world, separating land from water by speaking it into existence and order, then why would we question whether He could have or would have created the rest of the world into a mature livable state?

Scientists, some with their limited man-made philosophies and theories, would have us believe that the world has been here for millions of years and that our universe is perhaps billions of years old. I have a few problems with that logic.

First, consider the damage that we have already done in the briefly documented history of mankind. We have used innumerable resources, depleting some to critical low levels or completely. We have damaged our ozone layer. We have done countless things to contaminate our water, our air, and our land. If our earth is millions of years old, I truly believe that we would have destroyed it by now ourselves, or at the very least made it uninhabitable. Now, yes, I believe that if God exists, and I firmly believe that He does, He could have enlightened us to new energy sources, etc. to keep us going, as He does always provide. So, that's fine, assume I'm completely wrong here if you want.

Where is there any account of history that enables you to completely understand and account for the number of years the earth has been in existence? The ONLY place I know of is the Bible itself. If you don't believe in the Bible as a divine writing or instruction from God, then consider this from a historical perspective, because the Bible has proven to be very accurate concerning historical evidences.

There are actually a couple of ways of determining the age of our earth by using historical means in the Bible, and both result in the same timeframe. One is through historical events, and the other is through the documented genealogy.

Using Historical Events

Beginning with 0 (zero) A.D., and counting back to the archeological landmark event of the fall of Jerusalem, which has now been corrected to 588 B.C., instead of 586-587 B.C., then counting backwards the number of years prophesied between this event and the division of Solomon's kingdom (390 yrs. + 40 yrs., according to Ezekiel 4:4-7), would bring us to 1018 B.C.

Going from the end of Solomon's 40-year reign to the start of the Temple in the 4th year of his reign takes us back another 37 years to 1055 B.C.

Then, from the start of Solomon's Temple "in the 480th year", according to 1 Kings 6:1, back to the Exodus from Egypt (hence 479 years previous) brings us to about 1534 B.C.

The Exodus out of Egypt to Abraham's entering Canaan from Haran was exactly 430 years to the day, as we can gather from Genesis 12:10, Exodus 12:40, & Galatians 3:17, thus bringing us to around 1964 B.C.

Since Abraham entered Canaan at age 75, according to Genesis 12:4, he was born approximately 2039 B.C.

From Abraham's birth to Noah's grandson (Shem's son), Arpachshad's birth, 2 years after the Flood started, was 290 years, as we read in Genesis 11:11-26. This places the onset of the Flood at around 2331 B.C. Definitely in the range of 4,300-4,400 years ago.

In Pursuit...

The genealogy of Genesis 5:3-32 precludes any gaps due to its tightly structured chronology, thus giving us 1,656 years between Creation and the Flood, and bringing Creation Week back to near 3987 B.C., or approximately 4000 B.C.

Therefore, the biblical age of the Earth (using Scripture itself as a guide) is only about 6,000 years old!! According to this historically documented account, mankind did not evolve 4 million years ago on an Earth which is 4.5 billion years old in a universe which was "big-banged" into existence 18-20 billion years ago in the distant past. Jesus Christ, the Creator Incarnate, said He made mankind male and female in the beginning, in Mark 10:6, and that when the heavens and the earth were commanded into being, as read in Genesis 1:1, they "stood up together" (Isaiah 48:13) not billions of years apart !!

Using Genealogy

While we will discuss the genealogical method at length here, we will not delve into the individual "begets" that are listed in the Biblical Scriptures, but rather on the subject more from a whole context and deeper logical level.

As every student of the Sacred Scriptures is aware, the Bible contains lengthy genealogies. These records play a vital role in biblical literature, which is clear from the amount of space devoted to them in God's Word. Furthermore, they also provide a tremendous protection of the text via the message they tell. That message is this: **man has been on the Earth since the beginning, and that beginning was not very long ago**.

While genealogies and chronologies serve various functions in the literature of Scripture, one of their main purposes is to show the historical connection of great men to the unfolding of Jehovah's redemptive plan. These lists, therefore, form a connecting link from the earliest days of humanity to the completion of God's salvation system. In order for them to have any evidential value, the lists must be substantially complete.

An article on the subject from Apologetics Press continued with the following:

Yet some Bible believers—determined to incorporate evolutionary dating schemes into God's Word—have complained that the biblical genealogies may not be used for chronological purposes because they allegedly contain huge "gaps" that render them ineffective for that purpose. Donald England has suggested, for example: "Furthermore, it is a misuse of Biblical genealogies to attempt to date the origin of man by genealogy" (1983). John Clayton advocated the same view when he wrote: "Any attempt to ascribe a specific or even a general age to either man or the Earth from a Biblical standpoint is a grievous error". Clayton also stated: "The time of man's beginning is not even hinted at in the Bible. There is no possible way of determining when Adam was created".

In so commenting, most writers reference (as does Clayton) the nineteenth-century author, William H. Green (1890), whose writings on the genealogies usually are accepted uncritically—and acclaimed unjustifiably—by those whose intent is to insert "gaps" (of whatever size) into the biblical genealogies. Thus, we are asked to believe that the biblical genealogies are relatively useless in matters of chronology.

However, these same writers conspicuously avoid any examination of more recent material which has shown that certain portions of Green's work either were incomplete or inaccurate. And while references to the genealogies of Genesis 5 and 11 are commonplace, discussions of material from chapter 3 of Luke's Gospel appear to be quite rare. Two important points bear mentioning in regard to genealogical listings. First, to use the words of Custance:

"We are told again and again that some of these genealogies contain gaps: but what is never pointed out by those who lay the emphasis on these gaps, is that they only know of the existence of these gaps because the Bible elsewhere fills them in. How otherwise could one know of them? But if they are filled in, they are not gaps at all! Thus, in the final analysis the argument is completely without foundation."

If anyone wanted to find gaps in the biblical genealogies, it was Dr. Custance, who spent his entire adult life searching for a way to accommodate the Bible to an old-Earth scenario. Yet even he admitted that arguments alleging that the genealogies contain sizable gaps are unfounded.

Second, **even if there were gaps in the genealogies, there would not necessarily be gaps in the chronologies therein recorded. The question of chronology is not the same as that of genealogy**. This is a critical point that has been overlooked by those who suggest that the genealogies are useless in matters of chronology. The "more recent work" alluded to above as documenting the accuracy of the genealogies is from James B. Jordan, who reviewed Green's work and showed a number of his arguments to be untrustworthy. To quote Jordan:

"Gaps in genealogies, however, do not prove gaps in chronologies. The known gaps all occur in non-chronological genealogies. Moreover, even if there were gaps in the genealogies of Genesis 5 and 11, this would not affect the chronological information therein recorded, for even if Enosh were the great-grandson of Seth, it would still be the case that Seth was 105 years old when Enosh was born, according to a simple reading of the text. Thus, genealogy and chronology are distinct problems with distinct characteristics. They ought not to be confused."

Unfortunately, many who attempt to defend the concept of an ancient Earth **have** confused these two issues. For example, some have suggested that abridgment of the genealogies has occurred and that these genealogies therefore cannot be chronologies, when, in fact, exactly the opposite is true, as Jordan's work has documented. Matthew, for example, is at liberty to arrange his genealogy of Christ in three groups of 14 (making some omissions) because his record is derived from more complete lists available via the Old Covenant. In the genealogies of Genesis 5 and 11, remember also that the inclusion of the father's age at the time of his son's birth is wholly without meaning unless chronology is intended. Else why would the Holy Spirit provide such "irrelevant" information?

Plus, there are other important considerations. Observe the following in chart form. Speaking in round figures, from the present to Jesus was roughly 2,000 years—a figure obtainable via secular, historical documents. From Jesus to Abraham also was approximately 2,000 years—another figure that is verifiable historically.

Present to Jesus	2,000 years
Jesus to Abraham	2,000 years
Abraham to Adam	? years

The only figure missing is the one that represents the time period from Abraham to Adam. Since we know that Adam was the first man (1 Corinthians 15:45), and since we know as a result of Christ's testimony that man has been on the Earth "from the beginning of the creation" (Mark 10:6; cf. Romans 1:20-21), if it were possible to obtain the

In Pursuit...

figures for the length of time between Abraham and Adam we then would have chronological information providing the relative age of the Earth (since we also know that the Earth is only five days older than man—Genesis 1; Exodus 20:11; 31:17).

The figure representing the time span between Abraham and Adam, of course, is **not** obtainable from secular history (nor should we expect it to be) since large portions of those records were destroyed in the Great Flood (which interestingly enough is commonly believed to have happened, even by those 'non-believers'). But the figure **is** obtainable—via the biblical record. Allow me to explain.

First, few today would doubt the fact that from the present to Jesus has been approximately 2,000 years. [For our purpose here, it does not matter whether Christ is viewed as the Son of God since the discussion centers solely on the fact of His existence—something that secular history documents beyond doubt.]

Second, in Luke 3 the learned physician provided a genealogy that encompassed 55 generations spanning the distance between Jesus and

Abraham—a time frame that archaeology has shown covered roughly 2,000 years (see Kitchen and Douglas, 1982, p. 189).

Third, Luke documents that between Abraham and Adam there were only twenty generations. Thus, the chart now looks like this:

Present to Jesus	2,000 years
Jesus to Abraham	2,000 years (55 generations)
Abraham to Adam	? years (20 generations)

Since Genesis 5 provides the ages of the fathers at the time of the births of the sons between Abraham and Adam (thus providing chronological data), it becomes a simple matter to determine the approximate number of years involved. In round numbers, that figure is about 2,000 (see Arthur, 1999, p. 113). The chart then appears as follows:

Present to Jesus	2,000 years
Jesus to Abraham	2,000 years (55 generations)
Abraham to Adam	2,000 years (20 generations)

[The fact that **55** generations between Jesus and Abraham cover 2,000 years, while only **20** generations between Abraham and Adam cover the same 2,000 years, can be accounted for, of course, on the basis of the vast ages to which the patriarchs lived (see Thompson, 1995, pp. 265-275).]

Some have argued that there are sizable gaps in the genealogies (e.g., Clayton, 1980). But, where, exactly, should those gaps be placed, and how would they help? Observe the following. No one can place gaps between the present and the Lord's birth because secular history accurately records that age-information. No one can insert gaps between the Lord's birth and Abraham because secular history also accurately records that age-information. The only place one could put any "usable" gaps (usable in regard to extending the age of the Earth) would be in the 20 generations between Abraham and Adam. Yet notice that there are not actually 20 generations available for the insertion of gaps because Jude specifically stated that "Enoch was the **seventh from Adam**" (Jude 14). An examination of the Old Testament genealogies establishes the veracity of Jude's statement since, counting from Adam, Enoch **was** the seventh. Jude's statement thus provides divinely inspired testimony regarding the accuracy of the first seven names in Luke's genealogy—thereby leaving only 13 generations between which any gaps could be placed.

In a fascinating article several years ago, Wayne Jackson observed that in order to accommodate the biblical record **only as far back as the appearance of man's alleged evolutionary forebear** (approximately 3.6 million years), one would have to insert **291,125 years** in between **each** of the remaining 13 generations from Abraham to Adam as provided in Luke's genealogy (1978). It does not take an overdose of either biblical knowledge or common sense to see that this quickly becomes ludicrous in the extreme for two reasons. First, who could believe that the first seven of these generations are so **exact** while the last thirteen are so **inexact**? Is it proper biblical exegesis to suggest that the first seven listings are correct as written, but gaps covering more than a quarter of a million years may be inserted between each of the last thirteen? Second, what good would all of this do anyone? All it would accomplish is the establishment of a 3.6 **million** year-old Earth; yet old-Earth creationists, progressive creationists, and theistic evolutionists need a 4.6 **billion** year-old Earth. So, in effect, all of this insertion of "gaps" into the biblical text is much ado about nothing.

And therein lies the point. While it may be true on the one hand to say that an **exact** age of the Earth is unobtainable from the information contained within the genealogies, at the same time it is important to note that—using the best information available to us from Scripture—the genealogies hardly can be extended to anything much beyond 6,000 to 7,000 years. For someone to suggest that the genealogies do not contain legitimate chronological information, or that the genealogies somehow are so full of gaps as to render them useless, is to misrepresent the case and distort the facts; facts that are based largely on secular historical confirmation.

So, how old is our earth and universe? Even from a secular perspective, I would have to arrive closer to a 6,000 – 7,000 timeframe. So then, how do we explain the geological findings of multi-layered sediments and other factors that we believe date back millions of years? Catastrophic geology can explain many of these questions. The occurrence of the "Great Flood" is one example. Catastrophic events still happen; volcanoes erupting, earthquakes, floods, and other natural disasters. In all of these events, past and present, geological changes occur rapidly, unpredictably, and non-uniformly. Changes that may have taken hundreds or thousands of years, or may have never taken place, often occur in a matter of days, weeks, or months. How, therefore, can we accept the uniformitarian geological approach that certain earth-shaping and aging affects must occur over predetermined time periods when we factually know from present day experiences that this assumption is completely false? Uniform change would assume from the onset that no sudden or catastrophic events occur in order to "date" rock or strata formations. Even with the realization by some in the scientific community that some catastrophic events have occurred and some are recognized by scientists in geological dating of specific formations, we cannot be assured by any scientific methods that all events are noticed, recognized, or accurately interpreted. Nor can we assume that margins of error are small, since there is no documented evidence to support our man-made assumptions of geological dating.

So, to close on this point, there is far more logical and documented evidence available to us that the earth is only about 6,000 years old. Using that same logic and the statements made in the Bible, we can also find evidence that our entire universe "stood up together" at one time, already matured and ordered, just like man, woman, the birds, the fish, the plants, and the animals.

In Pursuit…

If you are still having a hard time conceptualizing or believing this logic, then also consider the "Great Flood" as another supporting factor. Since secular historians also have evidence of and believe that the "Great Flood" occurred, perhaps this will have more resonance for you. If the "Great Flood" happened, as we have evidence of, biblically and secularly, and all life on earth was at one time destroyed by this flood, how then do we account for all life now? The "Great Flood" only occurred a few thousand years ago, which does not leave enough time for the millions of years necessary for regeneration of complex life forms according to evolutionistic theory, such as humans, animals, etc. Therefore, we are led to believe that Noah's story of building an ark and carrying two of every kind of animal must be correct because we do exist today, as well as all of the animals, birds, etc… just a thought to consider in this closing.

So, just what if the Book is true? What impact will that have on your life, or your family's lives?

8 - So, What IF the Bible Is True?

Aw, the age-old dilemma… IF you admit and believe that the Bible really is true and real, then that means some serious lifestyle changes may be necessary, and that means being uncomfortable and maybe taking some comments from everyone we hang out with, and being embarrassed because nobody will believe the change will last. It means hard work, dedication to study and new learning, commitment to what we think we may now believe, and accountability to a higher Master than even our boss! Very un-cool… but is being cool now worth burning later? Believing in a hereafter is extremely difficult, while living for now seems much easier. It's your choice, but at least take the time to study and make an intelligent decision.

When you are looking to buy a new car, don't you look at several, inspect everything about them, study or research articles or reports about them, test drive them, and then make a decision? When you are buying a house, don't you look around, look inside, research how the home was built and by whom, study and ask about the quality and efficiency, consider the price, consider the future appreciation and value, and then make an intelligent decision? Of course!

In Pursuit…

Well then, that is all that I suggest to you now as well. Being in this world, you have heard of several religions, man-made theories, and atheistic views. Now I'm asking you to simply study and research the Bible on your own, look around, look inside, research how it was written and by whom, under whose authority, consider the price of believing or not believing, consider the future ramifications of the 'now' and the hereafter, then make an intelligent, well-informed decision on your own. Don't believe what someone is telling you. You have the source to study and find out for yourself. Study with an open mind and an open heart, putting all of the learned responses and prejudices aside for awhile. You don't want emotion and indoctrinated teachings to get in the way, you want to make a truly intelligent and well-informed decision, and you can't do that if you keep the mental baggage around to influence that decision.

What you study, contemplate on your own. Asking someone else that you frequently associate with will be a biased opinion based on their limited study, exposure, experiences, teaching and interpretations. You want a pure unbiased perspective, which only comes by self-study. Sure, you will have questions, and not everything may be crystal clear to you, but the basics, like what is absolutely right or absolutely wrong, or the plan of salvation that tells you about the promise God has made to you and how to accept it, these things are very plain and clear in the Bible.

As you study on your own, you may find yourself more inclined or interested in reading or listening to some things that teach or preach or talk about religious matters. In all of this I make one recommendation, consider these things from an earthly and man's perspective, not as the truth that the Bible will reveal. Also, as you have questions in your studies and research, remember that not every little detail that we question is a salvation point. What I mean is that even Paul, the writer of Corinthians as he wrote to the churches in Corinth, stated in I Corinthians 13:11, "When I was a child, I used to speak like a child, think like a child, reason like a child; when I became a man, I did away with childish things. For now we see in a mirror dimly, but then face to face; now I know in part, but then I will know fully just as I also have been fully known."

In other words, we will not understand everything now, but if we believe and are saved there will come a day after this physical life that all will be revealed to us. So many of the questions we have now

In Pursuit…
we will not be able to answer, which is where the whole faith issue comes into play.

Don't get too down on the whole faith idea quite yet. In order to have faith in anything or anyone you have to know it/them very well and have that trust that what is given to you from that source is true, makes sense, and is something that you can trust because it/they never contradicts what is told to you. "Faith comes by hearing", and hearing only comes from studying. Keep your prejudices about religious faith out of the way and just study with open eyes, ears, heart, and mind. See where that study does or does not lead you first on its own merits, write down or somehow note any questions that you do have as you move along.

After you're finished, then go find someone knowledgeable enough to answer them. Make sure that person knows and can support their answer from the same book, the Bible like that you studied from, though. You want supporting answers from the same source, otherwise, once again man's ideas and prejudices get interjected into what was a single pure source. Don't contaminate the Word with man's ideas. The whole idea behind you doing your own studying is to preserve the truth, weigh the message on its own merits, keep other men's views separate from what is a divinely inspired collection of writings, and make an unbiased life decision.

Now see? I'm not asking you to believe, nor pressuring you into any kind of Godly practice. All I'm suggesting to you, as the intelligent reader that you are, is to simply study and seek understanding of that book, then like every other decision that you make in your life, it will be a well-informed and intelligent decision.

I will say this, if you do take the time to seriously study and research the Bible, I do honestly think that it will change your entire outlook and lifestyle, as it is some powerful reading with an awesome message. In it, you will find action and adventure, science non-fiction that seems like science fiction, the dearest of romances, murders, sex, violence, peace, destruction, restoration, poetry, old proverbs, and history that is truly amazing. There is far more in the Bible than most people realize, and it has been the #1 selling Book for decades. Ever heard the story about the talking donkey? It's in there too!

This is the time for the hard decision. Do you start reading this book and studying it, which means other people may actually see you doing this, or might

In Pursuit…

hear you make a comment or two about it; or do you continue on in total ignorance because you're either afraid of what people will say, or you're afraid of what you may find that will put you in a moral dilemma of straight out denial and defiance or having to make the hard choice of changing your life's priorities? It's still your decision, but whichever way you choose, remember this as you breathe your last two or three breaths, someone just now offered you an opportunity to be ready for the last breath. How will you feel if you look back on this moment knowing that you had the chance to know, yet didn't take it?

You know, when that moment does come, and you are nearing your last breath of air on this earth, nothing else is going to matter to you at that moment. You won't be thinking about how many awesome cars you have, or the beautiful large home you own, or all of the "toys" and RV and fun stuff. Your only thought will be of that last gulp of air that you can suck into your lungs and whether you're really ready to meet your Creator or not as you let that last breath flow out of your mouth. Did you leave anything of value to your children, or spouse, or anyone on this earth? Not the "stuff", but something of spiritual value that will help prepare them for this same moment? These are sobering thoughts, but very real ones that we need to ask ourselves now, before that time arrives, and none of us know when that will be.

If the Bible, the Book, really is true; then that means that everything about Jesus is true; which means that His claims of being the Son of God is true. It also means that Jesus' death, burial, and resurrection would be true; which means that you better know who this Jesus fellow was, and is, and what He was teaching.

9 – Who Was This Jesus Guy Anyway? – Part 1

The Culture of Jesus
Part 1

Let's discuss who this Jesus was that we hear and read so much about. If there was some sort of intelligent design, and God is real, then so is Jesus and His life on this earth that is well documented throughout several historical accounts, including the Bible, is also real. With that stated, we need to know who this Jesus was, and is.

The purpose of this chapter is to offer an insight into the world and culture that we live in as compared to the culture that Jesus was in during His time on this earth. Also, to show our perspective as compared to His.

Often, we understand someone that we are listening to based upon what we know about that person, or "where they're coming from"... where they live, what they do for a living, are they single or married and with or without children, etc. This lesson is designed to give you a glimpse of "where Jesus was coming from" and where He was trying to lead our minds and spirits.

Too often, we overlook the simplicity of basic research when studying about Jesus. We are searching for complex answers and justification of our own lives as we study about Jesus, and are often limited by finite thinking and personal experiences. In order to understand "where Jesus was coming from", we need to return to the simple humanistic roots and traits of this man, whom we, as Christians, believe to be the Son of God.

As you read about the culture of Jesus, there are two distinct cultures about him to understand, the physical culture and the spiritual culture. The physical, or earthly culture of Jesus' day and time, is a return to the basics. You need to understand some of the basic cultural differences between Jesus' time, and ours, but also the specific differences between the Eastern and Western cultures that still exist even today. The physical culture helps us to understand "where Jesus was coming from", while the spiritual culture of Jesus tells us, in fact, "where Jesus came from" to impart upon this earthly journey. The spiritual culture of Jesus that will be presented in a subsequent section reveals what Jesus was trying to tell us about the spirit based upon examples of what we would understand by using the physical.

In Pursuit…

Now, let's revert back to strictly the physical culture of Jesus for the remainder of this section. As you read, I believe that you will begin to understand more about who the person of Jesus was and the relevancy of his teachings and examples here to us today.

Some of the following portions of this section are from a sermon preached some time ago by Ravi Zacharias, a Christian converted about 30 years ago from Hinduism, based upon some of his personal knowledge and experiences, as well as my own interjections from experience and study.

Interesting Points

In John 14:6, Jesus speaking to Thomas says, "I am the Way, and the Truth, and the Life. No one comes to the Father except through me." India, as we know it today, was one of the places that this same apostle Thomas visited... in fact, it was in what we now know as India where Thomas gave his life as a martyr, for boldly preaching about Jesus, and a memorial still stands in that country today. (This is interesting, since this is a country that worships 330 million gods, yet a memorial stands for the martyr of the One and only God.)

I worked with many "India" Indians and have been in some very interesting conversations with them. In many parts of the East, it is punishable by death if you change from your country's religion to Christianity... from Islam, or Hindu, or Buddha, or Bahaism to Christian is a certain death sentence. Whereas we, as U.S. citizens have the right to worship any religion, many countries in the east do not enjoy such freedom. In Jesus time, it was also a threatened environment, often times leading to death. In studying about the different apostles, you will find that Paul was often in fear for his life or in prison for preaching about Jesus. John was beheaded for his beliefs. Stephen was stoned to death. Others were beheaded or stoned to death for their belief and proclamation of Jesus as the Christ. While not always against specific laws of the day, certain powerful religious sects and political associations created a very dangerous threat for Christians in Jesus day. Even Jesus escaped some cities because he knew that some of these sought to kill him, and was not finished with the work He was here to accomplish.

Also remember the several passages that refer to multiple deities. Some had so many 'gods' and idols that they even had one dedicated to an "Unknown God". The east has literally millions of gods that are worshipped still today. Even of those of the same common beliefs, the conservative and extremist sects battle constantly. If we, who all believe in but one God, have disagreements and various interpretations, imagine how confusing it would be with millions of gods! The people in the East, therefore, tend to follow whatever their traditional family beliefs are because to research, study, and dispute them would be dangerous to their life, societal suicide, and would literally consume their entire life, and that of their children and grandchildren to arrive at any hint of religious origin.

Ravi Zacharias said this: "I came to Him because I did not know which way to turn. I have remained with Him because there is no other way that I wish to turn. I came to Him longing for something that I did not have. I remain with Him because I have something I will not trade. I came to Him as a stranger. I remain with Him in the most intimate of friendships. I came to Him unsure about the future. I remain with Him certain about my destiny. I came amid the thunderous cries of a culture that has 330 million deities. I remain with Him knowing that Truth (referring to John 14:6) cannot be all-inclusive. Truth by definition excludes all others." Powerful, powerful words and faith.

East vs. West

The East is very different from the West in how it establishes value. This is absolutely key in understanding where Jesus was coming from. In the East, using India as a prime example of Eastern perspective, first and foremost is the strength of the nuclear family... Father, mother, and children. This is true of most eastern cultures today, and was the same in Jesus time. The culture is strong and holds sacred the reverence of the immediate family. The bonds of the household are wrapped tightly in the East. So much, that the success or failure of the children socially elevates or lowers the entire family. Individuality is swallowed up by the clan.

This is such a vital point in eastern culture that every day, hundreds of advertisements are printed across the newspapers in what is called the "matrimonial section"... parents looking for spouses for their children. Every prospective bride and groom is advertised as being from "a good home" and searching for someone from "a good home". "My son is an engineer." "My daughter is a doctor." "My son was first in his class." "My daughter won a scholarship." The boasts run on at social gatherings. Everything is done to keep the family as a whole as a single unit, with complete and utter reverence for the parents' wishes on everything from jobs to marriage.

In Pursuit…

The second dimension, aside from the "glue" of the family ties, is the social reality of intense academic competition. Everything that defines an individual and his or her future is shaped by his or her performance in school. Every student wants to be the first in his or her class. It is not enough to just do well. You MUST be at the top of your class or close to it. Intellect is worshipped, and rewarded. This is relevant in that this is why we see the priests & scribes of Jesus' day holding the positions & power they had. They were regarded as very learned men for their time, the highly educated men of the day; whereas Jesus was simply a lowly carpenter's son, basically labeling Jesus as an uneducated or low educated man. Student's grades and position in the class are printed in the leading newspapers for all to see. In Jesus day, it was by word of mouth that this same information travelled. The simple fact that Jesus was a carpenter's son created the assumption in that culture that he was uneducated, thereby presenting a major challenge to Jesus' credibility from his very birth. Success or failure is reason for public pride or shame.

Ravi stated in one of his sermons that one man he knew said, "One of my closest friends toyed with suicide after his high school exams because he did not stand first in the entire city of New Delhi. Another one of my classmates in college actually burned himself to death because he did not make the grade."

If a father is in a high position, then his children are expected to achieve equal or greater social standing. A child's worth and perceived intellectual ability stem from the father's social position, and opportunities to the child are offered accordingly. Although the child can exceed expectations and restore pride to the family if the father is at a lower social level, the child can also permanently damage the entire family's social standing if they fall short. Obviously, this creates an extreme amount of pressure on the children to outperform their parents; which for those with parents of the highest standing in the communities dooms several to fail before they even start, for how do you exceed the highest standing?

This combination of the standard of the Home and the standard in Society is a volatile, yet core mix of the Eastern person's life. This value system is cherished with a passion, and very little has changed in this value system since Jesus' day.

Now, understanding the importance of Family and Social Academic standing, let's look at the <u>Culture of Jesus</u>, starting with Jesus' introduction; not as a baby in this world, but as the Lamb of God, the Messiah that every Jew had heard, studied, and prayed about all of their lives.

Can't you just imagine the conversation in the home of Andrew and Simon Peter, the earliest followers of Jesus, when Andrew first informed his family that he believed he had met the long-awaited Messiah? Here Andrew sits at the dinner table and he is saying that he just came from meeting the prophesied deliverer?! Any good Israelite had prayed for the coming of the One who could free His people all of their life, and now here this young man sits, saying that he has just spent hours with Him, and Andrew says he had even been given the opportunity to ask this Messiah any question he desired. Out of sheer curiosity, one at the table must have skeptically asked, "O.k., and what, perchance, did you ask Him?" "I asked Him where He lived," comes the confident reply.

Now, our response would probably have been something along the lines of, "You asked Him where He lived?!" Can't you just hear it from our perspective? "You what?! You get to ask the Messiah, the One who has come to save us, one question and that's the best you could come up with?!" We would have thought that question to have been a total waste of time, wouldn't we? This seems like a pretty casual & trivial question to ask the One who claims to be the Messiah, the One whom your grandparents, your parents, and you have prayed to come for generations, doesn't it? We would not care where He came from. Based on today's western culture, we would most likely want to know three basic things;

1. "Where is He?", because we would want to know the quickest route to get to him, and maybe even what to punch into our GPS system in our cars to eliminate traffic getting there. After all, we would want to verify this for ourselves, in person, or it's just hearsay.

2. "What can He do for me?", because we would need to mentally perform a cost analysis to at least ballpark the ROI, Return On Investment, since we would be spending time and money to get there and see Him ,and those two items (time and money) are precious to us in western society.

3. "How fast can He do it for me?", as our assumption would be that if we spend the time to get there and grace Him with our presence, there better be some good old-fashioned U.S.- expected instant gratification awaiting us.

The more I have thought about it, though, the more I am convinced that this would-be disciple had very sound reasons for asking what he did, especially in that eastern culture. This was the beginning of Andrew's serious investigation into the person of Jesus. Was this truly the Christ, the Anointed One? For nearly 2,000 years, the prophets had told of His coming.

The Setting of the Question

The setting is given in the 1st chapter of John. Immediately, we notice the casualness with which Jesus made His entry. There is no drumbeat, no great fanfare or parades, nothing to herald the coming of the One whose name would be on the lips of humanity in a way that no other name had ever been, nor ever has since. These people expected an earthly king that would finally, once and for all, take them to the top of the status food chain over the Romans and the rest of the known world. They wanted everyone to hear, see, and know that they had just been promoted to the top of the societal totem pole. Yet, Jesus came into action gently and almost silently compared to what the people expected.

John the Baptist, or baptizer, was given the honor of making the unadorned announcement. John, draped in strange clothing (even for his day) and living off of even stranger food, was gaining a huge following. In the eyes of the devout, he was a prophet of supreme honor. Yet for John to have proclaimed this carpenter's son from Nazareth as the Messiah was even stranger. No "king-maker" could have ever conceived such a modest approach for such a world-changing announcement, especially not in the East!

Yet, on that day at a divinely appointed moment, Jesus came to John to be baptized. Awe-stricken by this privilege, John stuttered out his own unworthiness of such an honor, declaring that he was not even fit to untie the sandals of his Lord. The scene is memorialized even to this day, however, by the dove descending upon Jesus. As this heavenly affirmation was given, John looked at two of his own followers and said, "Look, the Lamb of God."

Think about this. This was a sobering statement from John the baptizer. The average Jewish family grew up with lambs and sacrifices. The temple probably reeked of animals and their slaughter, especially on the Day of Atonement. The exterior grandeur of the temple housed only a rather grim and messy alter. So, stating that this Messiah was the lamb of anything was even an unexpected and very unappealing concept. Every lamb sacrificed was a lamb of men offered to God. It wasn't an equal to men, not a representative from among men, just a dumb unsuspecting animal brought into the temple, never to return.

Now, in this appointed moment in history, an offering came from God Himself and was given by God on behalf of Humanity... the Lamb of God. One born for the purpose of being sacrificed on the alter someday. Yet, even with this grim picture of who this Messiah was, these followers of John who heard his pronouncement of Jesus as the Lamb of God turned from John to follow Jesus. You see, they knew and understood what this meant; the impact and greatness of this statement in that culture. For generations, men had sacrificed lambs to God; now, God was sacrificing a Lamb for men. If they understood the spiritual impact of that statement, they followed Him. If they failed to understand that one simple statement for the spiritual victory that it meant to them, they rebelled against Him.

Now, back to Andrew... wouldn't this jolting introduction by John the baptizer, a respected supreme prophet, have provoked or inspired a different question from someone wanting to become a disciple of the Messiah? Remember the assertion that I made earlier, that in the East, the home is the defining cultural indicator. Everything that determines who you are and what your future holds is tied to your heritage and your social academic standing... absolutely everything. You see, in Jesus culture, the East, Andrew's question was quite typical, and vitally important to these people in determining someone's value or worth as a person.

It's not at all surprising that Nathanial's response when he was told about Jesus was, "Can anything good come out of Nazareth?" And some verses later, "Is this not the son of Joseph, the carpenter?" How in the name of reason could the answer to the hopes and dreams and prayers of Israel, in search of a Messiah, come from a city of such low esteem and from a family of such modest professional status? The best way for them to find out whether He could really be who John described Him to be was to follow Him to His house - to the earthly address of the One who claimed to be the Son of God.

Jesus' answer to Andrew's question, "Where do you live?" builds the intrigue. He didn't give a street name or house identification. He simply said "Come and see." So, Andrew followed Him to where He was staying and evidently stays the night there. When he returns, Andrew tells his brother Simon and invites him to "Come and see" also.

The next day, Philip, who was also from the same city, invited Nathanial to join them, saying, "We have

In Pursuit…
found the one Moses wrote about in the Law, and
about whom the prophets also wrote - Jesus of
Nazareth, the son of Joseph." There you have it again
- the city and the parentage. After hearing that,
Nathanial is skeptical and cynical, and given the same
challenge, "Come and see."

Now, here is a people who have been hearing
about, praying for, and looking for this great Messiah,
the Savior of their people, the King of Kings... man,
they're ready for a major blow-out power party and
trumpets blowing and all the pomp and circumstance
of the most powerful King ever known to come save
their day... and here is this poor man that walks up,
from the "wrong side of the tracks", dirty from
walking in the dry hot desert, hair ratty and tangled
and dusty, and we are told that He was not spectacular
or incredibly handsome... the son of just some
carpenter that some of them know from this city that
isn't regarded with much respect socially, and he
walks up and claims to be the King of Kings, the
Messiah that you've listened to your grandparents,
your parents, and teachers talk about as a great
hero...this is the Lamb of God, God's Son, the Hope of
Hopes that we've been waiting on?

As important as His earthly parentage was, especially to these people in this culture, His home address was not an earthly one. From John, the same writer that we get the record of Andrew's question from, the Gospel writer forthrightly states this in John 1:1 & 14: "In the beginning was the Word (which we know is Jesus), and the Word was with God, and the Word was God... and the Word became flesh and made His dwelling among us."

The "Lamb of God" in a very real sense, had no beginning, as we understand beginnings in our mortal realm. Amid the "where" and "when" questions that plagued these people, and plague us today, there is no such encumbrance for the eternal and infinite One. We will look at more of this in the article on the Spiritual Culture of Jesus. He had an eternal perspective that He was trying to elevate them to throughout His teachings. Yet, He had to teach His message through earthly ideas within their culture that they could understand and relate to. Sometimes when we say that we just don't understand the Bible, it is really because we haven't taken the time to understand the culture that Jesus lived in or was teaching in.

The task ahead of Jesus when asked where He lived and He told them, "Come and see", was to lift them beyond the here and now. Beyond the limited understanding of this world and truly show them how to follow Him home... to His home in Heaven.

In Pursuit…

Andrew had a reason for asking the question, and Jesus was offering a journey of thought as His answer. We will take that journey farther in Part 2 of this lesson, but for now, put yourself in Andrew's sandals. He had been invited to the home of the One identified by a recognized prophet as the Lamb of God.

Now, to us today, would you recognize Jesus if He walked up to you? Would you recognize a Jewish, dirty, sweaty, poor man in torn filthy clothing and sandals with no real earthly belongings, what we consider as financially broke and destitute, as your Lord and Savior who has the power to forgive your sins and mistakes? Would you bow down at his feet, before this one called Jesus, in your dress pants and gold watch and nice hair and sweet smell? Would you worship Him and accept Him as He is, and believe Him when He speaks to you? Would you look at Him and try to be just like Him?

How about if He took you by the hand and said, "Here, stand with me. Let me look at you. I love you, do you know that? That's why I hurt for you. That's why I cry for you. That's why I died that day for you. I'm so glad that you can finally really see me." Would you ask, "Where do you live?" Would you want to follow Him home?

Jesus is still telling us today the same thing that He told Andrew ,hoping that we, too, will understand the importance of that question, and the relevance of His answer... "Come and see."

10 – Who Was This Jesus Guy Anyway? – Part 2

<u>The Culture of Jesus</u>
Part 2

<u>The Culture of Jesus</u> Part 2- The Divine Culture

Part 1 was 'The Physical Culture of Jesus'.

Part 2 is 'The Divine Culture'.

In Part 1, the physical culture of Jesus helped us to understand "where Jesus was coming from" in an earthly sense. In this article, we will begin to explore "where Jesus came from", a very different perspective. Herein, we will begin to look at who Jesus really was. Each of us has our earthly roots, yet He had ascended from a culture far beyond what we could imagine; a divine culture that truly defined who this Master was and is to us.

Jesus only purpose on this earth was to reach out to us at our own level and tell us what His home not of this earth was like, and to invite us there by enabling us to become like Him, pure and cleansed in spirit, through His death and sacrifice for us. As we begin to learn about Jesus' divine culture, let's remember His physical culture. This enables us to better understand His words as we progress.

Some portions of this article are from a sermon preached some time ago by Ravi Zacharias, a Christian converted about 30 years ago from Hinduism, based upon some of his personal knowledge and experiences, as well as my own experiences and study.

Part 1 - Review of the Physical Culture

- Family Ties - Exceptionally strong in the East and Middle East cultures. The clan swallows up individuality, meaning that what is best for the family/family name far outweighs any personal needs.
- Social/Academic Status - Intellect is worshipped. Must be in the Top of their Class or very close to it, doing well is not good enough.
- The people in Jesus day had been looking for a Messiah, a King, someone to save them from their current "status" for generations. Had been prophesied about for 2,000 years.
- Then John the Baptist introduces this man called Jesus, from Nazareth (a city of low esteem, wrong side of the tracks), and the son

In Pursuit…

of Joseph, a carpenter (low family professional status).

- These people were raised with sheep, and bloody sacrifices of their lambs.
- Jesus is introduced as the "Lamb of God".
- New thought is introduced that most understood the impact of, but few understood the real concept of... men sacrificing lambs (animals) to God was one thing, but now God sacrificing His Lamb (His Son) for men' was an entirely different concept.
- Andrew's question upon meeting this proclaimed Messiah, "Where do you live?" & the importance of that question in their culture for defining the social and political authority of a person.
- Jesus' reply "Come and see", the purpose being to begin showing Andrew and the other followers the spiritual home & authority that He came from, not the earthly home.
- Jesus' task was to lead them on a journey of thought, beyond the here and now, that would enable them to truly understand how He would deliver them according to the prophesies.
- Nathanael's response to Jesus - before meeting Him. His skepticism and cynicism with

comments like, "Can anything good come from Nazareth?," and "Isn't He the son of Joseph the carpenter?"

Now - Part 2 - The Divine Culture

- Jesus' task was to introduce the eternal perspective of thought and heart that they had never had to consider with their earthly ways of sacrifice and traditional worship. He had to establish a personal responsibility for salvation within them and separate the family interest from the individual need to follow Him.
- Nathanael's response to Jesus upon meeting Him, and Jesus' response to Nathanael demonstrate this in the first chapter of John.

John 1:47-51: Jesus saw Nathanael coming toward Him, and said of him, "Behold, an Israelite indeed, in whom is no deceit!" Nathanael said to Him, "How do You know me?" Jesus answered and said to him, "Before Philip called you, when you were under the fig tree, I saw you." Nathanael answered and said to Him, "Rabbi, You are the Son of God! You are the King of Israel!" Jesus answered and said to him, "Because I said to you, 'I saw you under the fig tree,' do you believe? You will see greater things than these." And He said to him, "Most assuredly, I say to you, hereafter you shall see heaven open, and the angels of God ascending and descending upon the Son of Man."

Jesus had seen Nathanael when Nathanael didn't even know he was being watched. In one of David's psalms, David confessed that he could not flee from God's presence, for God knew him in his inmost being: Psalms 139:7-10 "Wherever I go, You are there." Nathanael had just realized the same truth. Jesus also knew that Nathanael didn't think very much of Nazareth. Recognizing what was in his heart, when Nathanael said "Rabbi, You are the Son of God! You are the King of Israel!" Jesus challenged him and said "You believe because I told you I saw you under a fig tree. You shall see greater things than that... I tell you the truth, you shall see heaven open, and the angels of God ascending and descending on the Son of Man." John 1:50-51

Jesus, in short, said, "You are shocked because I revealed you to yourself? Wait until you see the full truth of who I am and where I come from!" He took Nathanael from explaining the lesser things to a destination of glorious insights. Jesus establishes a very personal knowledge of each of these who approach Him from their first sight of Him.

We just read about Nathaniel, and just before this, He has a similar encounter with Simon; John 1:41-42, He (Andrew) first found his own brother Simon, and said to him, "We have found the Messiah" (which is translated, the Christ). And he brought him to Jesus. Now when Jesus looked at him, He said, "You are Simon the son of Jonah. You shall be called Cephas" (which is translated, A Stone). Stop here for just a moment and note the parentage reference, "son of Jonah". The physical culture is always an important key point to remember when studying the Bible or the life of Jesus.

Back to the scripture, this is the same Simon that we see in **Matthew 16:13-18, where it says:** *Now when Jesus came into the district of Caesarea Philippi, He was asking His disciples, "Who do people say that the Son of Man is?" And they said, "Some say John the Baptist; and others, Elijah; but still others, Jeremiah, or one of the prophets." He said to them, "But who do you say that I am?" Simon Peter answered, "You are the Christ, the Son of the living God."*

And Jesus said to him, "Blessed are you, Simon Barjona, because flesh and blood did not reveal this to you, but My Father who is in heaven. I also say to you that you are Peter, and upon this rock I will build

In Pursuit…
My church; and the gates of Hades will not overpower it.

Note the parentage references again; "Son of the Living God", "Simon Bar-Jonah", "My Father who is in Heaven". There's a consistent reference to parentage & heritage throughout these scriptures.

Jesus used this worldly understanding of culture to lead the apostles to realize & understand His divine cultural roots. And now, blessed is Simon Peter for recognizing the true parentage of Jesus, for taking that journey of thought and faith to a place beyond the here and now, and seeing Jesus as God's Son, not Joseph the carpenter's son or Jesus of Nazareth.

Here in John the first chapter, we have the account of Simon first meeting Jesus and Jesus calls him Cephas, which means "stone"; then here in Matthew's account, in an event that happens later between Jesus and Simon, we see Jesus calling him Peter, meaning "rock", because of the confession that Simon, now Simon Peter, has so boldly proclaimed. The confession, which Jesus says is the rock upon which He will build His church, comes from Simon, whom

He called Cephas , or "stone", when they first met. Do you see the divine connection here?

Jesus knew these men & the roles they would each have before they ever came to Him. Just like He knew Nathanael before he came to Jesus... and just like He knows us before we come to Him. This divine journey of thought that He took them on is something that He still beckons us to come on as well. Yet, as long as we continue to think with the physical limits of when & where & time that bind us like slaves on this earth, we will never be able to understand or submit to the limitless, eternal, boundless joy of freedom that is in Christ and in God.

To be like Christ; to teach others; to live according to God's will; to even understand our own salvation, we have to understand that our thinking MUST change to an eternal perspective and see things from Heaven's point of view, not the world's... "putting off the old man and putting on the new man" as we are told in Ephesians and Colossians. It is then, and ONLY then that can we prioritize our life, our goals, our work, and our purpose according to God's purpose for us as individuals, each with our own gifts to offer in His service. If we hope to ever attain happiness and cease pursuing it, we must understand and live by that eternal perspective. In the U.S., our constitution gives us the right to life, liberty, and the

In Pursuit…

pursuit of happiness; and now globally, through God and our Savior, Jesus the Christ, we have the hope of attaining it; because the Bible, the "Book", gives us that right and enablement. The constitution gives us the right to pursue it. The sacrifice and Word of God gives us the ability to attain it.

I believe that Jesus came as a vision of our perceived earthly weakness in order for us to understand God's strength and power over all that we know in our limited minds. Anyone would have expected a great and glorious King on this earth to be socially & politically strong and have influential parents and live a high lifestyle, and even more so in the eastern culture. We would expect Him to have the ability to get laws changed and be powerful enough to deliver them, because that's the way the world thinks. But He wanted us to think the way that God thinks; the eternal perspective; the "forever with Him" concept, instead of placing value among the things of this earth that will pass away. So, He came in a very unexpected way so that we could see God in Him, and know Him for who He really is, not for what He has or how He looks. Have you ever noticed that we are never given a detailed physical description of Jesus?

He wanted us to see His heart, the heart of God, not a physical form.

It was through His earthly disadvantages that we are shown God's conquering advantages. By showing us how much He could do in God against what we thought were all odds, Jesus revealed to us how little we can do in ourselves, no matter how great we think we are. Through His strength to overcome every temptation, every evil, even death, was revealed the true level of our weaknesses and our true need of a Savior, a sacrifice that we could NEVER make.

Have you ever asked God, like Andrew did, "Where do you live?"... or cried out "Where are you?", only to discover that He lives within you, everywhere you go He is there just waiting for you to follow Him home? Have you ever asked, like Nathanael, "Can anything good come from this?", and then found out later that He knew you before you knew Him? Have you ever figured out that in all of your struggles, He was already shaping you into that person that you would have to become to serve him in the role that He already knew you would take?

Our culture perishes; this earthly, physical culture that we know, whether from the East or the West. The culture of the world is dying each and every day. It had a beginning, and it will have a definite end. There

In Pursuit…

is time, and space, and motion... and all of these earthly-defined boundaries, yet, it all fades and decays with every passing minute. The reality you know right now is temporary. You sitting here right now is only a blink of an eye... a mist... a vapor, then it's over and you're gone from this earth, never to return and no second chances. You are doing **now** all you will **ever** get to do on this earth. This may be your last minutes. Do you ever think about that? Do you live every day, every moment, like it is your last?

Our culture perishes, but, Jesus' home lasts forever. It is renewed with the glory of God's presence forever. There was no beginning, and therefore will have no end. There are no bounds, no limits of time, nor space, nor motion. It comes closer to being your **only** reality every second, and is certain to overcome & replace the reality that you know and understand right now, regardless of how hard you resist it or how rich or poor you are.

Whether you like it or not, whether you're ready or not... Eternity is coming. Death is coming, as a welcomed promotion if you're one of His faithful children in spiritual battle every day, but either way, Death is coming to take you home. It's only a bad thing if you're not ready. Place your value, the things that matter to you, in God's house, and it will all be yours to claim and keep forever. Place your value anywhere else, and you will claim nothing... your whole life will be lost and wasted with nothing to show for it and no hope forever.

When you meet this Jesus that we have learned more about, which culture will He know that you place value in? Have you boldly proclaimed Him as God's Son, as his apostles and other believers did, no matter what the cost on this temporary earth, because your riches are stored eternally? Or have you continued to see Him as Jesus of Nazareth, son of Joseph, the carpenter, as His enemies did right up to His death? Are you thinking from His home, or from yours? While He is watching you now, even when you don't think about it, what does He see in you? As other people are watching you, even when you don't realize it, do they see Him in you?

Consider this last thought... In God's eyes, there is no staying neutral to avoid conflict. He says that either you love Him and despise Satan, or you love Satan and despise Him. You are either for Him or against Him... Against Him, you will die. For Him, you will live beyond anything you can possibly imagine. You cannot serve two masters. There is no such position as neutral. There is no such thing as an

In Pursuit…
undercover Christian. There is no such thing as a
silent warrior in the heat of the battle.

11 – Transcript of God's Sovereignty

The recurring theme throughout all of this so far seems to be this intelligent designer, a Supreme Father of all things. So, who is He? Who do I suggest is this Creator that could create such things and what is He capable of? Well, read on and I'll try to explain a little more about Him. Being the created, I can only define my Creator to a certain degree, that which I am able in my finite knowledge and wisdom. However, here is some beginning anyway.

"Sovereignty" means Supreme Excellence or Supreme Power. Let me start by sharing a short story that we'll use to make a critical point. There's a doctor's son, Matt, who is a sophomore in college now. He's participating in a program in Irian Jaya. It's called "The Edge Adventure." That's a small, fairly-new program, and academically, it's really quite rigorous. The students probably write more papers in this semester than they do if they were at home. But the papers are written out in longhand, and they're written mostly by candlelight. Yet, most of the learning, as you might imagine, doesn't happen in the classroom, but instead comes from living among "Stone-Age" people and being fully immersed in a totally different perspective and culture.

In Pursuit…

Matt was only able to call home once in the first three months. The first thing he mentioned was about the mail service. It is notoriously unreliable. Both Linda, his mom, and Laurie, his girlfriend, have sent him dozens, even scores of letters, but, for a time, Matt hadn't gotten any mail for about five weeks. Realizing in advance that this was going to be the situation, Linda and Laurie numbered their letters sequentially so that Matt would know if he's getting his mail, and if he's getting it in a timely fashion. And Matt says he got Laurie's letter number seven and then five weeks later he got her letter number 22. He didn't know what was in letters eight through 21, but when he read letter number 22, he knew that everything was okay. See, the details could be filled in later.

This strikes me as a picture of our lives as well. We've read the first seven letters. We know where we've been. But we don't know yet what will be in letter number eight. So we worry about it. These things are in the future. That's the tomorrow, and some of the days ahead look very challenging, I think, for us.

Some of us worry about our kids. Like, how are they going to turn out? Some of us worry about college costs, and we hope desperately that Christ returns before we have to start paying for the university. Almost all of us worry about the future of medicine and the challenges that face us there. But the good news is the Good News. God's a postman. He's already delivered letter number 22 to each of us in his own handwriting through the scriptures.

And this is what my letter said. He said, "Brant, you'll be happy to know that it all turns out just fine." God's not making specific promises to us that life might not be tough in the interim, but He does say this: "You can trust me. You can trust my power. You can trust my care. It will all end just fine." The sovereignty (supreme excellence, supreme power) of God is in the rest of our lives.

Perhaps by now some of you have seen or heard about this little note. I ran across it from hearing a speaker mention it once. I want to share this with you because there's more tonnage of importance per square millimeter in this than you can possibly imagine. And this is what it says:

"Good morning. This is God. I will be handling all your problems today. I will not need your help. So have a good day."

Think about it. Memorize it. Say it every morning before you get out of bed.

In Pursuit…

I want to draw your attention to three passages of Scripture. You can turn to them, if you want, but I'll kind of summarize them fairly quickly. The first is Psalm 37. I'll give you segments of verses one through eight. It says:

"Do not fret because of evil men or be envious of those who do wrong. Trust in the Lord and do good. Delight yourself in the Lord and he will give you the desires of your heart. Commit your way to the Lord. Trust in him and He will do this. He will make your righteousness shine like the dawn, the justice of your cause like the noon-day sun. Be still before the Lord and wait patiently for him. Do not fret when men succeed in their ways. Do not fret. It only leads to evil."

Now three times in those eight verses it says, "Do not fret." What does that mean when it says, "Do not fret?" It means, don't fret! Matthew 6:33& 34:

"Seek first the kingdom of God and his righteousness and all these things will be added unto you." 6:34 says, "Do not worry about tomorrow for tomorrow will worry about itself. Each day has enough trouble of its own."

Now what does that mean when it says, "Do not worry about tomorrow?" What it means is, don't worry! Philippians 4:6, it says:

"Don't be anxious about anything, but in everything by prayer and petition with thanksgiving, present your requests to God."

My question is, what does it mean when it says, "Don't be anxious?" It means don't be anxious!

Now we read those passages and we say, *"Aren't those comforting verses? Isn't that wonderful of God to provide us that encouragement right at our point of need?"* And we get up from our table, we walk out in the hall and we start worrying, and we start fretting, and we start being anxious. We all do it — 100 percent of the people that you know do it. And yet, the Scripture says, "Don't. Just Trust me. Be still. Wait patiently for me. The reason you worry is you don't know who I am. You just don't see clearly enough yet."

There's a favorite verse of mine. It happens to be in 1 Corinthians 13. I don't know how this gets slid into the "love chapter," but it says,

"Now we see through a glass darkly, but then we shall see face to face. Now we know in part, but then we shall know, even as we also are known."

127

In Pursuit…

What if we could go to the other side of eternity, beyond the line of eternity, and just sit in the presence of God for 10 minutes, just 10 minutes, and then come back here and finish out the rest of our lives? Would it change the rest of your life if you had 10 minutes to do that? It would change everything! The change would be total, and it would be complete.

To try to just catch a small glimpse of what this would be like, think about this scenario. A small town is so incredibly close to God, He decided to invite one of us up for a look… kind of a once-in-eternity opportunity here. I'm not allowed to tell you who it was, because you're supposed to notice the difference in him yourself when he gets back, but we'll call him Joe. Actually, he's up there right now, and I want to tell you what Joe's going through.

See, here's Joe sitting with God. And this is what he says first to God, "God, I've got 10 minutes here with you, so let me ask you this: Do you know everything?" And God says, "Do you doubt it?" Joe says, "Well… well, no, but how do you do it? Doesn't it all get kind of mixed up in your head?" And God says, "I think you're getting the two of us confused there, Joe. You do that a lot, you know? You really shouldn't do that so much. Let me put it this way: Things get mixed up and chaotic in your head a lot, but not in mine. Joe, my car never runs out of gas. I've never been late for a plane. And when you try to balance the checkbook… every time you sit down to do it, I just can't bear to watch. So I distract myself by counting backwards… to infinity."

Joe says, "Could I see you answer some prayers?"

"Sure."

"Well then?"

"I just did."

"Did what?"

"I just answered prayers."

"Well, whose prayers did you answer?"

"Well, actually, Joe, I just answered 924,000 prayers just then. Half the time people don't even know I'm doing it. I'm kind of tricky about some of this. A very high percentage of the prayers I answer are not even from adults. It's the kids, you know? They're the ones with the faith. When I answer their prayers, they usually see it right away."

In Pursuit…

"Well, what percentage of prayers, that you just answered right now were from kids?"

"Well, to be precise, 42.57688493005998729609432547…"

"That's enough," Joe says. "That's enough."

Joe says, "How many stars are there?" God says, "Joe, you only have 10 minutes."

"Well, how many galaxies then?"

"Joe, you only have 10 minutes. But do you want to see me annihilate an entire galaxy?"

"Oh, sure, cool, that'd be great!"

"Well, you see that one way out there toward the edge of space? It hasn't been discovered yet. Nobody will even miss it. I just made it because I liked the way it sparkled. Watch this. There, you can't see it now, right?"

"How'd you do that?"

"You don't want to know, Joe. Ever heard of anti-matter?"

Joe says," I am a physician, you know." God says, "Is that supposed to impress me? I'm a physician, too. You want to compare credentials? Success rates? Diagnostic accuracy? Pick a topic, any topic."

Joe: "How much time do I have left?" God: "Just a few seconds. But of course, around here that costs me 50 trillion years, but in your case, it's just a few seconds."

Joe: "Do you watch me all the time?"

"Sure, I do. Other people sometimes watch you, too. You're really quite an entertaining fellow."

Joe: "Medicine is getting kind of stressful these days."

"Yeah, so I noticed."

"What should I do about it?"

"Well, Joe… I'm glad you asked. One thing that would help a lot is if you were to stop using me as a last resort. Everything you need I've already provided. Trust me. Use my wisdom. Use my power. Pray. Joe, you really need to pray more. And love your patients. On your best day, I'll give you a great day. On your worst days, I'll get you through it. I will always get you through it."

"God, one last question. How do I get down from here?"

Joe: "Oh, I guess that was a really silly question. Hi, Honey. You'll never guess what just happened to me."

Joe's wife: "What? You looked sunburned. You've been golfing again?"

"Oh, no, no, it's not golfing. Maybe you'd better sit down. I'll tell you about it, but first, I think we'd better pray."

How would you walk the rest of your life? Everything that you do, every attitude that you had, every thought, every opinion about people and about time and about eternity and about human effort would be changed! Now, we can't go to the other side and sit with God for 10 minutes, but we can know a lot more about him than we have previously settled for. And the best way, perhaps the only way, to go into an uncertain future is to trust in the sovereignty and the power and the majesty and the precision and the genius and the intimacy and the caring of an almighty God. No other approach will work. No other approach makes any sense whatsoever. And He says, "Put your hand in my hand and don't let go, not even for a second."

Let's look at some things that we know in medicine and astronomy and in physics, about the sovereignty of God. Think of the sun. If you took a pin head and you heated the head of that pin to the temperature of the core of the sun, it would kill every person within 1,000 miles. Did you hear that?

Now let me ask you this: Could God hold and play with, or even swallow that pin? Yes! Now somebody that is that powerful, what does that tell you about your ability to trust him in terms of his ability to do things that we can't even begin to imagine? Everything that you see out there in science and in astronomy and in cosmology or in quantum mechanics or in the human body or biology or chemistry or physics — God's fingerprints are all over it. And He's teaching us that we can trust him.

Let's look at black holes. Consider God and black holes. All galaxies have black holes. Our Milky Way galaxy apparently has many of them. The number of black holes in the universe might even be larger than the number of visible stars. To get a feeling for how intense a black hole is, to make a star into a black hole, you'd have to collapse the radius of our sun from 450,000 miles down to two miles, so it could pretty much fit in a small town, okay? Now, a sun that had that kind of density would weigh more per teaspoon than Mount Everest does. That's what a black hole would be.

This isn't just an academic exercise. This teaches us about God, and you'd better listen because you're going to need this God in your future. We all are going to need a God that has this kind of power, and we can trust Him.

You know, as you get closer to a black hole, you finally get to the event horizon — what is called the event horizon. If you step one inch further, then you're gone. Nothing can escape once it's entered the event horizon.

I wonder, does God sometimes stand on the event horizon and sort of taunt a black hole? I mean, what happens if He sort of slips over the edge a little bit? Who wins in that tug of war? God or the black hole? God wins! You see, there is nothing in the universe, there is nothing of created order that is more powerful than God. He created it all. He controls it all. He overpowers it all.

Well, think of that. It is an amazing thing. It's fun thinking about God and how He bullies the universe. I mean, He just does whatever He wants to do whenever He wants to do it. Now a God who's that powerful, can He handle your problems? Does He even need your help?

Let's look at numbers. What kind of mathematician is God? Do you know that the number of electrons that pass through a filament of an ordinary light bulb in a minute...did you get that? The number of electrons that pass through an ordinary filament of a light bulb in one minute equals the number of drops of water that flow over Niagara Falls in a century. Does God know how many electrons flow through a filament of a light bulb in one minute? He does. He counts them in his spare time. Do you know there's 10 to the 80th elementary particles — protons, neutrons, electrons — in the observable universe? That's 10 with 80 zeroes behind it! 1 Billion has 9 zeroes… we're talking a total of 80 zeroes here as the number of protons, neutrons, and electrons in the observable universe… and we only observe a very small part. And God has every one of them mapped, every nanosecond. He nicknames them in His spare time.

In Pursuit…

The talking number — they call the talking number — it's the number of words spoken by humans since the dawn of time, which we know is about 6,000 years. Did God hear all of those? It's 10 to the 16th, and growing every second! Did God hear all of those? Yes, He did. He's got a record of them.

The Coney Island number. Do you know what the Coney Island number is? It's 10 to the 20th. It's the number of grains of sand on the Coney Island beach —10 to the 20th. Does God know all those little grains of sand? Yes, He does. The Ice Age numbers — 10 to the 30th. That's the number of snow crystals necessary to form the Ice Age. Does God do math at this level? Yes, He does.

I want to talk about the human body a little bit because my time is running out for this chapter. The human body has 10,000 trillion trillion atoms. That's greater than the number of stars in the universe. A trillion of these atoms are replaced every one millionth of a second. Every one millionth of a second, in your body more than one trillion atoms are replaced. Even though our bodies are indeed discrete units, we leak. Physically and metaphysically, we leak. In consequence, we share our physical existence with our neighbors, however remote.

In the last one hour a trillion trillion of your atoms turned over. That's not a typo… that's a trillion trillion! What happened to those atoms? Look at your neighbor. That's where they are. Your neighbor's got them now. These atoms float off into space and then they roost in your neighbor for awhile — red, and yellow, black, and white. They are me and I am them. You might not like that, but it's the truth of the matter. Through common breathing, shared sneezes, sloughed skin, the jet stream, flowing rivers, and a myriad of other mixing devices, God brings us together, constantly and continuously. God has them all mapped. He knows where they all are. He follows them around, and it's the way He designed us and our world… we are truly all one; all the same, despite our differences, and He loves us all equally.

Take a deep breath. Everybody take a deep breath. When you do that you just inhaled 150 million air molecules that Jesus breathed. I didn't read this from a Christian book. I read it from a physics book. The math is very well worked out. Email me, but I still won't be able to explain it to you. It's far beyond the math that I understand! Take a deep breath again — 150 million air molecules that Jesus breathed. I choose to view this as Jesus doing mouth-to-mouth resuscitation on me all the time. My advice to you, if you want to do something you don't want Jesus to be a part of, you better hold your breath.

Every cell has a trillion atoms. Okay, you've got the little tiny atoms and then you've got the cell. Every cell has about a trillion atoms. Well, we have anywhere from 10 to 100 trillion cells in the human body. And you guessed it. We're making over a trillion cells every day. The lining of your GI tract turns over about every two days, (faster if you eat Mexican food!). The lining of our skin turns over every two to four weeks, and I read recently that the average human being sloughs like 40 pounds of skin in a lifetime. (Maybe that's why old sofas weigh so much!)

Red blood cells… You make 2-to-10 million red blood cells every second. If you take your red blood cells out and line them side by side, they'd go round the earth at the equator four times. You think God paused when He made the red blood cell? I think He did, knowing that His son would have to shed this for the remission of our sins. Now, I don't want to overly spiritualize that, but did one of Jesus' red blood cells have my name on it? What's the divine value of one red blood cell? Is that sufficient to cover all of my sins? I think it is. This is the God that we serve.

And this God is a capable God. And this is the kind of God who is not only powerful, He is not only precise, He is not only a mathematician…The level of precision in a created order like our universe is 10 to the 10th to the 127th. That's impossible. There are no numbers like that — 10 to the 10th to the 127th , this is how precise our God's power and order are… this is perfection… this is supreme excellence and supreme power. And this is the God that we serve. This is the one that you can actually talk to and get to call Father… like your daddy here on earth, but this awesome, unstoppable, force of incredible power and Love, is your Father waiting for you in Heaven!

Why don't we trust Him more? Why don't we pray and talk to Him more? Why do we balance the whole thing on our shoulders? We can't do that! You & I can't even control just our own thoughts most of the time! And yet He gently and so calmly says, "Don't worry… don't fret… don't be anxious… Trust me. Lean on me. Take my hand, hold on to me, and don't let go for even a second. I will get you through everything just fine." He is so gracious. He is so patient. He is so intimate. He is so personal. He created us because He loves us, because He wants a relationship with us, and because He wants His glory to be seen by us and in us, and because He wants us to move-in and live with Him in His city and see Him every day. You and me… feeble, nothing, powerless, weak you and I… with that God… our Father. What an awesome, unbelievable thought and invitation!

You know, the unbelievers will tell us that if they see it, then they'll believe it. I say to them, no… if you believe it, then you will see it. Jump and the net will appear! *"Faith cometh by hearing, and hearing from the Word of God."* "Faith is the essence of things hoped for, and the evidence of things not seen."

They say we must be crazy to believe in God… I say, anyone who has this kind of evidence of God's fingerprints everywhere around them, in them, on them, and permeating every possible facet of their little lives and still doesn't believe, now that's crazy… and sad… and inspires our mission to teach all that much more. "For faith without works is dead." Our teaching others is our work. That's what I mean…there is no Christian cruise control.

So how do your works become works of faith, and how does all that determine where I'm going with my life?

12 - Factors of Light

The premise of the four Factors of Light that I mentioned earlier, and will present here, is found in these passages.

Matthew 13:11 & 12; *"Jesus answered them, 'To you it has been granted to know the mysteries of the kingdom of heaven, but to them it has not been granted. For whoever has, to him more shall be given, and he will have an abundance; but whoever does not have, even what he has shall be taken away from him.'"*

Matthew 25:28 & 29; *"Therefore take away the talent from him, and give it to the one who has the ten talents. For to everyone who has, more shall be given, and he will have an abundance; but from the one who does not have, even what he does have shall be taken away."*

There are four basic Factors of Light to consider when thinking about where you have been, where you are, and where you may be going in your walk, whether you feel that to be a spiritual walk right now or not. All of these are important factors to consider now as you move forward in this book. Be honest with yourself in deciding where you believe

In Pursuit…

you are now. Without knowing where you are, you will never know where you're going.

In **John 12:46**, Jesus said, *"I have come as Light into the world, so that everyone who believes in Me will not remain in darkness."*

So then, Light means Jesus and knowing Jesus and His purpose, and, in my humble opinion, the right way to live; whereas Darkness means NOT knowing or accepting Jesus, nor His purpose, nor the right way to live. Alright, with those explained, the four basic Factors of Light are as follows;

Factors of Light
1. Revelation
2. Refusal
3. Reception
4. Reckoning

Factor 1 - Revelation
Revelation is defined in the most basic sense as being our conscience. It is that natural sense of light and darkness, right and wrong, that we all are inherently born with. Although conditional stimuli in our various up bringing can distort this sense to some degree or another, most of us in our right mind know

some basic light and darkness, or right and wrong. We know when we are being mean to a person or when we are being nice. We know an insult from a compliment, and so on. Granted, some people may think that doing the wrong thing is acceptable behavior, or in their surroundings and based upon their younger experiences and/or mentors that some wrong behaviors are 'normal', but that does not negate the fact that if they are in their right mind they still know that their behavior is wrong. A perception, even a misperception, that something is acceptable or 'normal' does not equal a perception of right behavior or choices versus wrong behavior or choices. So again, the Revelation Factor presumes that we are all born with a basic sense of right and wrong, our conscience.

Alright, this is where the dishonest doubter gets the term dishonest. They are dishonest with themselves, because they refuse to admit that our conscience is in anyway related to inherency. They want to believe that it comes strictly from circumstantial, situational, conditional stimuli, and that there is nothing natural about having a conscience. Of course, this renders every opportunity to discuss anything different with them futile, thereby stopping their course dead in its tracks right here. You might as well quit talking, because they are not in a position in their life, yet, to where they are willing to listen to anything spiritual.

Factor 2 - Refusal

Revelation can lead to Factor 2 or 3. Factor 2 is refusal, which is defined as refusal to accept the revelation of light. It is the refusal to acknowledge and live by that small amount of light that we are all given. This is part of what makes these words in the scriptures above have so much meaning; *"…but from the one who does not have, even what he does have shall be taken away."* How can something be taken away that does not exist in at least a small part? Jesus was telling us something about ourselves in this, that each of us is given some light. Whether we choose to acknowledge it and make it grow is our choice. **By refusing the light, you increase the darkness for yourself;** *"…even what he does have shall be taken away."* Now, understand, there are many things that can lead a person to refusal, and the devil is behind every single one of them. Satan knows his job, and does it well! Just a few of the things that can lead someone to the refusal of acknowledging their own conscience would be greed, mistrust, evil companions, a need for acceptance, or peer pressure – even if they don't believe these people are evil companions, and lack of exposure to other light – which, by the way, is where you & I come into action for God by spreading the Gospel and reaching out, fellow Christian! We don't fish in a bathtub and expect to catch fish, so why would we think that we can only preach the Gospel to other Christians at chuch and reach the lost?!

Factor 3 – Reception

Revelation can also lead to Factor 3, Reception. Reception is just that, a person who acknowledges and receives willingly that small portion of light revealed to them through their conscience. **Accepting the light, increases the light**; *"...For whoever has, to him more shall be given, and he will have an abundance...."* After reading Refusal and Reception, you may have the misconception that I am saying that a person who chooses Refusal is forever lost. Not by any means! He or she is only lost as long as they continue to choose to refuse. I believe that the reason Jesus said that they would lose what they did have was simply a statement of faith, saying that if a person chooses NOT to receive what little light he or she has been given, and if they CHOOSE to refuse to acknowledge that light, the natural progression would be to move farther away from it. Everything that we are taught in the Bible shows distinct sides, you are either with God or against Him. Therefore, there is no standing still; and therefore, no being on middle ground. We are either moving toward Him or away from Him, toward the light or away from it.

Factor 4 – Reckoning

Reckoning is that moment that we choose. It is that moment of realization that the Truth we seek is in the light, or in the Light. Your reckoning will come either way, but concerning your continuing on to learn from this book, or even more importantly the Bible, which is where I hope this leads you, your reckoning is when enough Light enters into you to cause that change necessary to make you act on the knowledge you gain in the Truth. It is that moment that you decide to make the changes necessary in your life to put you into God's service, and motivate you to act upon your newly found faith and make yourself an obedient follower of Christ.

You may be at this moment of reckoning right now, or have already passed this moment in your spiritual life. If so, then that is a truly wonderful place to be, and I sincerely hope that you will continue reading to deepen your faith and grow even more. *"…For whoever has, to him more shall be given, and he will have an abundance…"*

If you are not at this moment of reckoning yet, I hope that you will continue to read on and STUDY YOUR BIBLE! Don't just read it, STUDY it intensely! Hopefully, something I can say within the walls of this message will motivate you, intrigue you, inspire you, or do whatever it takes to get you to open the Book that really matters, the One that WILL get you to this point in your life!

Now, for those of you who now believe that you have that 'warm fuzzy' you were so searching for, remember this passage, as well, as you carry on forward;

Luke 12:47-49

"And that slave who knew his master's will and did not get ready or act in accord with his will, will receive many lashes, but the one who did not know it, and committed deeds worthy of a flogging, will receive but few. From everyone who has been given much, much will be required; and to whom they entrusted much, of him they will ask all the more."

To those of us who have been blessed enough to know the Word, we have much required of us. Even as we learn more, we have increasingly more required of us. Bear that in mind as you move on throughout your Christian life and studies. We are required to live, love, and share the Light, the Gospel.

In Pursuit...

I am convinced that on our Day of Judgment, if we are truly Christians always truly seeking and earnestly trying to walk in the Light, according to God's will and the pattern of Jesus life, our stumbling and remaining sins will be covered by the blood of Jesus; and that we will NOT be judged according to those sins, since they will be covered, but that we WILL be judged according to our Light and how we chose to use it or hide it in our lives, how we chose to share that Light, the Gospel. We need to believe that we maintain our salvation through striving to walk in the Light. *"If we walk in the light, as he is in the light, we have fellowship with one another, and the blood of Jesus, his Son, continues to cleanse us from all sin."* **1 John 1:7.** Jesus said that He came to seek and to save the lost! If we are to also seek and to save the lost, we can only find them and show them the way in a dark world through His Light! If we are hiding that Light, then we aren't sharing the Word; and if we aren't sharing the Word, we are ineffective Christians, and of no use to God on the battlefield.

Matthew 13:37-42, Jesus was explaining the parables He had spoken in previous verses to His apostles, *And He said, "The one who sows the good seed is the Son of Man, and the field is the world; and as for the good* *seed, these are the sons of the kingdom; and the tares are the sons of the evil one; and the enemy who sowed them is the devil, and the harvest is the end of the age; and the reapers are angels. So just as the tares are gathered up and burned with fire, so shall it be at the end of the age."*

"The Son of Man will send forth His angels, and they will gather out of His kingdom all stumbling blocks, and those who commit lawlessness, and will throw them into the furnace of fire; in that place there will be weeping and gnashing of teeth."

We are either the good seed or the tares. We either spread the Good News, the good seed, or we sow the tares and become stumbling blocks. Jesus doesn't define any middle ground here or in any other scriptures, but on the contrary, makes it very clear in ALL other passages that there is NO middle ground. So, Christian, beware and prepare. Know the God whom you serve and serve Him fully and completely, not half-heartedly nor in complacency. Anything less than fully is incomplete, and in contempt.

13 – Liberalism vs. Biblical Truth
(A Warning!!)

This chapter is important after the earlier discussion about religious disunity and finding Truth in the Bible. The church and its worship, in the group or 'corporate' sense, is very clearly defined in doctrine; yet many congregations are gradually adopting 'new' thinking or practices, many of which are bordering, leading to, or have stepped over the doctrinally defined commands of acceptable worship, as commanded.

These congregations have begun to compromise their beliefs in order to grow in numbers. They seek more mass appeal by giving in to social peer pressures. Small steps have led to large divisions in the body that have resulted in more social confusion and distorted negative perceptions about Christianity and God's Word. Although there are several issues alive and well within the church, since we are, after all, still human and subject to Satan's ability to deceive, liberal thinking instead of biblical thinking is one of the chief causes of disunity and division.

Liberalism

Liberalism: The wide acceptance of individual lifestyles, beliefs, and practices; not necessarily subscribing to their beliefs or theories, but accepting the individual choice of lifestyles, beliefs, and practices.

The definition self-identifies some of the dangers of this value system. Therefore, I am going to address Liberalism from a 'church' perspective.

Liberalism is treacherous, especially in the church, but really in any aspect of life. Liberalism begins most times with sincere motivation, yet lost focus. Focus, however, requires dedicated concentration and adherence to specific predefined boundaries. Liberal thinking, of course, does not. Liberalism is equal to or results in mass acceptance of unquestioned and unchallenged practices and acts, thereby creating less stress and decreased synaptic resource usage in the brain, while eliminating confrontational or useful need for Absolute Truth.

The inception of liberal thinking generally occurs when a person loses the value of the truth that they believe in. The person feels that since they have the truth embedded in their daily life, they can now serve to make it better or more attractive and acceptable to others. The goal is usually twofold; first, self-serving, to create something new and exciting from what has become familiar, routine, and mundane; second, to 'reach' more people in hopes of growing the person's beliefs to the local populous and perhaps beyond.

Utilizing liberalism to deliver you from boredom can be invigorating, but crippling. The 'new' will soon become routine also, so another 'new' is introduced… then another, and another, etc. These small, seemingly harmless new practices and acceptances quickly distract or completely change the person's original focus on truth, soon totally redefining the person's beliefs as the person attempts to justify their new position on what they know is the absolute truth.

The amazing growth stimulated by liberal acceptance, thinking, and practices becomes simply a smoke and mirrors act to attract others. The overwhelming success experienced is complete deception, because the truth and beliefs that the person sought to share initially are no longer the pure truth of what founded their beliefs; only a muddy contaminated version that was created for marketing, rather than the pure divinely created Truth to save.

Those who are receptive to the 'new' liberalized truth are being deceived into believing what they perceive as an easily accepted truth, as you market it as such; which requires no change in thinking or lifestyle for them. They perceive from you an "easy" or "quick save," justification, and "no forgiveness needed" type of salvation... a quick fix for wider social acceptance. The divine reality is that they are lost because they do not know the Truth and do not want to know it; or know the Truth and have rejected it, hence their acceptance of your liberally contaminated "no action required" version being presented.

Each small step in liberal thinking or acceptance is like inching towards a black hole. Remember that discussion? Each step seems harmless enough, just an inch closer to the event horizon... until that last inch when the black hole sucks you in, and before you realize where you are or that anything happened, you are processed into a different person, place, and thought. You have stepped one step closer to the cliff... or have you stepped off?

Biblical Truth

Biblical Truth: The absolute adherence to doctrinal understanding of worship grounded strictly

In Pursuit...

in God and His Word; not *"added to nor taken away from,"* but exactly as instructed within the contexts of the Bible and the New Testament church's example.

Worship is offered to the glory of God, in Christ, by the Spirit for the edification of the church. The order of this statement is vitally important. God is the object of worship, and worship must be God-centered, not man-centered. This is a key point in closely monitoring the introduction of liberalism into the worship. If one goes to worship for what he can 'get out of it,' that person is going for the wrong reason. We go to give glory to God. We are drawn by gratitude for what God has done for us in Christ, not because of the acceptance of a more attractive doctrine or worship method. Spiritual benefits for the individual worshippers certainly result, and the principal means by which the church is built up in the faith is the corporate services of worship.

The doctrinal understanding of worship must be grounded in God. Worship is determined by the nature of God. One of the most profound descriptions of worship is found in John 4:21-24. Since God is Spirit, worship must be *"in spirit and in truth,"* meaning that worship must be spiritual and real (the Greek word for "truth" here suggests "reality"). Worship must be genuine and true, and if we begin instating practices or thoughts of a more liberal nature, our worship can be neither of these. Since God is the creator and sustainer of all life, the creature (created) must come before God on God's terms. The basic attitude must be one of humility.

Paul bases his instructions on the corporate conduct of worship in 1 Corinthians 11 on the order of nature established by creation itself. This provides doctrinal explanation for the position assigned to women in worship. Women's activity in the church is restricted in public worship. (1 Cor. 14:34ff; 1 Tim. 2:11ff are descriptions of public worship). Subordination in this **one** aspect, or sphere, is probably due to the nature of worship. Worship is addressed to the Creator; hence one observes the order of creation, man first, then woman. One comes to God as his Maker, or he does not worship God (Heb. 11:3, 6).

The specific character of the worship of the church is governed by the fact that it is "*in Christ.*" Christ's (Jesus) body is the new temple (John 2:19). He is "*the Truth*" (John 14:16). The Christian comes to God not only as Creator but as the Father of Jesus Christ. Redemption has given a new relationship with God and a new motivation for worship. Thus,

In Pursuit…

Christian worship is directly related to the "name of Christ." The church is a divine institution with a divine mission. Our worship and behavior are not works to earn our way into Heaven, but outward manifestations of our faith and obedience as commanded and instructed in scripture.

Liberalism & Biblical Truth Cocktail

Trying to mix liberalism into biblical truth, doctrine, or worship is much like combining oil and gasoline into the purest of waters. It appears so beautiful with so many swirling changing colors, like a liquid rainbow that can mesmerize anyone watching. Yet they will never actually combine, and all are rendered useless. The oil and gasoline are no good for use with the water present, nor is the water fit for human or non-human consumption; much like worship is not presentable or acceptable to God if contaminated by man's ideas, no matter how attractive it has been presented. Worship must be in spirit and truth, as we have already discussed. If man introduces more liberal ideas into the worship service because he thinks that it will provide some added benefit for the worshippers, then it is no longer in truth as prescribed in the scriptures.

The mix can be intoxicating to those that see it and participate in it, yet if they are not worshipping according to scripture, then they are not worshipping. God is the Creator. We are the created. Worship to the Creator by the created is to be on His terms, not ours.

Liberalism is not some giant roaring beast that we see coming. It is a series of small stings that sometimes go unnoticed, yet will eventually lead to the disablement or death of a congregation, or at least to the perceived truth that they claim to be teaching. Many times, elders will strive diligently to find that "safe" balance of adhering to scripture, but adding or allowing or trying one small something new to re-engage members and/or attract potential new members. Many times they justify the action by the reports and/or observations that other churches are engaging these practices in worship, perhaps even attracting members away from their church. So, one small move at a time, seeing what they perceive as positive results to the congregation, they lead the whole church step by step farther away from the biblical truth and closer to that event horizon.

Let me assure you that as clearly as the sky is blue and grass is green, there is no "safe" balance! The only safe balance is 100% biblical practice of worship and no tolerance for the introduction of anything not specifically presented within scripture. If

In Pursuit…

it is man's or men's ideas, it has no place in the worship of our God. Just as some of the burnt offerings that were offered up to God in the Old Testament were not acceptable nor recognized by God; worship according to man's terms may help appease man, making him feel better and justifying his unrighteous life, but that worship is not acceptable nor recognized by God. True Christians don't want to just feel good or have a "warm fuzzy" about their life, but rather seek the full knowledge and confidence that when they die, they want to feel saved and know they have a home with their Creator awaiting them.

Please do not be deceived by those who offer anything different from what the Bible teaches, whether in doctrine, nor in worship. Study the New Testament church; their preaching, their teaching, their singing, their communion (memorial of Jesus death), their confessions, their giving… understand those examples of worship given by Jesus and His apostles. See the apostolic church in its entirety and whole context, and seek to follow that example and become a part of that worship with a congregation that teaches and practices that Truth, nothing more and nothing less.

14 – The Pursuit of Happiness

This is a short chapter, but a powerful thought, so stay with me here.

"*We hold these truths to be self-evident, that all men are created equal, that they are endowed by their Creator with certain unalienable Rights, that among these are Life, Liberty and the pursuit of Happiness.*" (from the Declaration of Independence)

You know, as I sit here writing in our garage on my laptop; as it is the only place that I can sometimes escape the chaos of our four children; surrounded by boxes of rarely, if ever, used things, and stored items that "we just had to have", it inspires me to write this chapter on our great right in "*pursuit of happiness*".

We love animals. We have four dogs, and one cat. At one time, we had 15 animals in our home, but have since down-sized a bit. Children are attracted to our smallest dog, Dipsy, a little double dapple wiener dog. They are drawn to her like her hair gravitates toward my pants. They pursue her. And she runs away. So they chase her all the harder. And she goes to even greater lengths to escape - hiding under the bed, climbing the leg of my pants (with leg still inside).

In Pursuit…

It is not that Dipsy the dog does not like to be petted. She loves it! But, being a wiener dog, which all seem to have very distinct personalities, she prefers that any contact with humans be completely on her terms. So, when pursued by a stranger or new person, she runs away.

If, on the other hand, a visitor to our home tries to ignore Dipsy, doing something obviously other-focused like reading the newspaper, our guest will soon find a rather spoiled little dog camped out in his/her lap insisting on being petted.

The pursuit of happiness may be a right, but it's also futile. Happiness is a dog. Chase it and it will run from you. Forget about it and focus on more important things, however, and joy will soon be sitting in your lap.

Do we chase happiness? I think so. We work more and more so we can buy more and more so we can experience more and go more. But are we actually enjoying any of it anymore?

If we aren't catching long-term happiness, maybe it's time to stop chasing it. Perhaps we need to re-evaluate our approach and learn from a little dog. Better yet, we should learn from one who learned from God.

In a short book long on its emphasis on joy, the apostle Paul offers practical advice for achieving happiness. He had discovered the secret of being content, and found it to be independent of his circumstances (see Phil. 4:12) "*Each of you,*" he explains, "*should look not only to your own interests, but also to the interests of others.*" (Phil. 2:4).

It seems that is another way of saying, "Don't chase the dog. Stop trying so hard to be happy. Stop focusing on your happiness and re-focus on others. When you forget trying to find your own happiness, it will then find you."

Here I am, recently diagnosed with a non-fatal, but disabling disease, unable to work full-time in my previous profession of over 20 years, and wondering how we are going to survive this crisis… yet I am incredibly happy. How is that?

My first thoughts are my wife and children. I think of my 8 year old little girl, Tatiana, and my 9 year old son Isaac. Most nights, about 3 or 4 in the morning,

In Pursuit…

they navigate through a toy covered floor in the dark and into our room, sneaking quietly into our bed and snuggling up with Mom and Dad. I think of my two older sons, Jacob, 14, and Joshua, 16. They try so hard sometimes to be grown up, yet those dependencies on Mom and Dad still surface, even when they don't want to show it.

My wife, Sara, 16 years younger than I, so excitable and high strung is so opposite my extremely conservative and quiet behavior. Yet that is exactly what makes us so perfect together. Our differences complement one another and give us new strengths through one another.

My family means everything to me, and I love each one dearly for who they are. I know that each one has the foundational beliefs that will lead them safely through this life, even when they make mistakes and fall short sometimes, as we all do. God has blessed me greatly.

We may have struggles, but more than that we have a love that binds us together that is greater than any one of us individually. And we have a love for God that binds us together eternally. Our struggles I leave to God, laying them down before His throne, because I know that I cannot fix everything that is challenging us right now, but He can. As my father always said with a deep conviction, "God will provide", and He will. My father also said often, "This too shall pass", and it shall.

So, how can I be happy in this time of extreme struggle and life challenges? By two simple realizations, I can attain peace.

First, understanding that I cannot fix everything right now and laying these burdens down for God to carry for me, as I know that my Father can fix all of our hurts, and through Jesus as my mediator, God understands clearly.

Second, focusing on what really matters. It's not all of the "stuff", not the things or the "pursuit" of happiness, but the realization that I'm not pursuing it… it's beside me in bed every night, and with me every day. It's my family, the people that God has placed in my life that really matter, and my love for Him. They will be here no matter what I have or don't have. They have needs far beyond what money can provide, and I still have a job, a responsibility, and an opportunity to change lives. I still have the command to provide for them, even with a disability; so, I provide all that I am able to in their lives, and God provides avenues for providing the rest. I still have

In Pursuit…

contact with many other people that I touch and influence in so many ways. I'm not pursuing happiness, I have it sitting in my lap craving attention, craving direction, craving acceptance. Happiness has been given to me on a silver platter, everything else is just "stuff".

Stop pursuing and start appreciating. Stop pursuing and open your eyes to what you already have surrounding you. You can't store people away. They are growing, they are going, and they are pleading inside for you to love and accept them, direct them, and protect them.

Life, liberty, and the pursuit of happiness- having the right doesn't make it right.

15 – In Pursuit - Happiness vs. Joy

"Rejoice in the Lord always: and again I say, Rejoice." Philippians 4:4

Happiness is joyful, but joy doesn't always equal happiness. We can find joy in many circumstances and situations, not all of which are happy times. Happiness comes from outside circumstances, some of which we control and many that we don't. Joy comes from within, which we do control completely. So, for example, it's cruel to say to people who are in sorrow, "Smile, and be happy." It's better to come alongside and mourn with them than to try and force the square peg of happiness into a round hole of sorrow. The human life is a life of tragedy, sorrow, heartache, and pain. Yet in every difficulty, you can find joy. Happiness is an outside job. Joy is an inside job.

We arrive again at that pondering question, what does God have to do with it? And again the same answer applies... everything! Look at our own society and those in it. There are real estate tycoons who own half of New York City's business districts and computer software moguls that are struggling to find real happiness. This is not to say that all of these

In Pursuit…

people are miserable, but they are still in pursuit of what will fulfill them. They have everything in the world within their grasp, and most of these things in their possession already, yet the pursuit is still in motion. Most have not attained what they seek from within, although they have attained all that they seek from an outward desire. The same can be said of the poverty stricken, as well, except they want outwardly and need from within.

When you acquire new things or attain certain levels of achievement, based upon the tangible world around you, you feel a sense of happiness. This feeling, the emotion of happiness, has been born of external circumstances. Unfortunately, the feeling is short-lived, leaving you with the desire or need to get more or do more to receive its brief reward again. This is one of the chief reasons we see our global culture accepting the misconception of marriage so readily. The world now perceives marriage as a test drive. If it all works out without any inconveniences or problems, it's the extreme exception. In most cases, it is a lease, not a purchase. It's now acceptable to marry for awhile, even pre-planning for the nearly inevitable failure with prenuptial agreements.

Our society has become so confused about who they are and where we came from that people and their emotions are considered disposable. It has become completely okay to use people for pleasure and toss them aside like trash. Where and when did we become so terribly out of step with God? We cherish things, use people, and pursue the unattainable. Somewhere in our cultural evolution into this heartless, self-serving, joy-starved society, we have forgotten the difference between happiness and joy. We seek joy by attaining moments of happiness, when happiness is only really attained through sustained joy.

Joy is that mystical creature that lurks somewhere deep in all of our hearts, just waiting to surface, but seldom seen. Some will even argue that joy doesn't really exist, but those very same people are those who have lost the true definitions of happiness and joy, wallowing in their self-made pity prisons lacking either one. Others will tell you that they feel joy every time they find a new partner or purchase something new or achieve a certain new status level, but these are the truly confused folks. They haven't lost the definitions, but sadly confuse the two.

Joy is only achieved when we can become content in where we are, yet knowing and still striving for where we are going. Joy is brought about by inner commitment to appreciate where we are now, and by re-establishing correct values. Joy understands that the people in your life are irreplaceable, even those who may be a thorn in your side sometimes. Joy understands that it takes constant, consistent, concentrated effort to love and be loved. Joy is derived from an inner perspective, not outward circumstances. Joy isn't planning your future, but living it. It's not getting married, but staying married. It's not in having children, but in raising them.

Everything that brings true joy also brings heartache at some point. Sounds strange, doesn't it? But consider, how would we know up, if there were no down? How would we know right, without a left? How would you know good without bad, or hot without cold, or tired from rested, and on and on? You cannot know joy, without heartache, because one leads to the other and back again. This is how we grow and mature. This is how we become able and qualified to instruct others. Joy knows contentment. Joy knows peace. Joy knows truth, the absolute Truth that leads to joy. Joy knows gut-wrenching heartache and hard work. Joy knows attainment of happiness, again and again, even in less than happy circumstances. If in struggles, joy sees growth and opportunity to learn and become better. If in happy moments, joy appreciates the reprieve from the struggles of this life.

Like love, joy is also a decision. It is a decision to persevere; to improvise, adapt, and overcome the negatives and reach through to the other side and grip only the positives. Joy is an inward expression of praise to the Maker that becomes evident outwardly. Joy is the light that we shine to the world, showing them that it is possible, it is real, and it is attainable. In Matthew 5:15-16, Jesus said, *"Neither do people light a lamp and put it under a bowl. Instead they put it on its stand, and it gives light to everyone in the house. In the same way, let your light shine before men, that they may see your good deeds and praise your Father in heaven."* Notice something here blatantly obvious for us to understand? The scripture says "YOUR good deeds", which means effort and action on your part; then your good deeds are for whom to be praised? Is it for you to be praised, for accomplishing such kind and wonderful things? No! Your good deeds are for men to see and "praise your Father in heaven". Joy knows service; Leading other people by service to other people, to lead them to praise your Father in heaven. Joy knows God, for God alone is the source for true and lasting joy. The world is in pursuit, while God is offering attainment.

16 – In Pursuit – Contentment & Relationship

Contentment, and especially in a Relationship, seems nearly impossible, doesn't it? It seems almost Hollywood, like the ending of a good movie where you see the man and woman finally getting together, but never see the life that follows; just the realization and pinnacle of their love finally being spoken and affirmed. It's the 'happily ever after' syndrome, as if the moment is being exited during that happy time, not bringing into reality the struggles that are inevitable, or the decisions they make to either keep or break their promises to one another in the relationship later.

So, is contentment or a lasting relationship really attainable now, like our grandparents or parents relationships were? Or is all of that just an old-fashioned pipedream now? How did they do it? What in the world could keep two people together, pure and undefiled in that kind of relationship for 50, 60, or even more years? And just because they stayed together that long, was it really in contentment, or just pure stubborn determination stirred with a little misery and discontent? These are some of the questions that we will seek to answer in this chapter, along with if and how this kind of relationship is still possible. Please, open your hearts and minds as you continue reading. If you think with the world's view, you will be blind to the message given within.

The answer in short form is a resounding "YES! Contentment CAN be found in any relationship." In our society, a lasting relationship is considered amazing and old-fashioned because it requires values that are now old-fashioned. It takes remarkable maturity to develop the patience, kindness, longsuffering, and love that is required to sustain an earthly relationship. In fact, to sustain such an earthly relationship requires a strong spiritual relationship.

Aw… so there we have it. Spiritual relationships have become, for a large part, an unacceptable compromise in our lives. To have a spiritual relationship with any pronounced deity requires that we openly admit a dependence upon that deity to at least some degree. Dependency is considered a weakness. We have been taught from a very early age that our success or failure depends upon us individually. We have been indoctrinated with a world view that we are the sole creators of our own destiny, and to take on that responsibility.

In Pursuit…

While that may be true to some extent, it is not within the same limits as it once was. When our parents or grandparents were taught these same principles, there was an underlying value system and assumption that God was in the equation. Today, that same assumption is conspicuously absent. As I explained in the preface of this book, it has been an observation and proven ideology through numerous studies conducted by many organizations of Christian and secular association that people in our country, and indeed our entire society's foundational structure has been transformed into a convenience-oriented, self-seeking, very confused society of non-thinkers.

We have allowed a select few that we have consciously or unconsciously crowned as authorities to mold us and shape us, injecting their thoughts into our minds and making us believe that it is our own original thoughts of accepted societal moral absolutes that we believe, then bending us towards the thought of no moral absolutes except as defined by each individual person, therefore rendering 'right' and 'wrong' as ineffective ideals.

We have allowed media, music, and the confused separation of politics and religion to shape our beliefs into a stir pot of melted mass individualism. Yet that individualism is a mass-mentality at its base, thereby growing a herded culture of open-mindedness and wide-acceptance of very twisted and perverted beliefs where adherence to those principles that our country was founded upon are now perceived as religious imprisonment, rather than the freedom that allowed us to form a separate nation.

So by and large, the very core values and beliefs that once governed our behaviors and moral conscience are now regarded as self-imposed prisons that only the weak hide in and cling to in order to justify their failures or lack of motivation to achieve great success. With that perception, relationships are optional, providing us with temporary fleshly satisfaction and a right of ownership over the other person until we feel hindered in our progress towards the ultimate goal of achieving success or our perceived happiness, which is always found to be as lacking as the temporary relationships that we had getting us to that point.

The purpose of all of this is simple, to bring out the truth again that we have been culturally programmed to love things and use people. Until that perception changes, we will continue to see many of the same relational issues that we face today, yet even worsening. To attain the same lasting relationships

In Pursuit…

and contentment that we saw in our past, we each, as individuals, need to become individuals in changing our society's beliefs. Our society and culture will only change as a majority when change in one person at a time begins to occur. When you become you, instead of being a part of your surroundings, then we will begin to see the positive changes in our current mass-mentality. Masses only consist of many individuals, therefore, if the individuals begin to change perceptions of right and wrong by re-instituting absolute truths and moral absolutes based upon biblical principles, the masses will begin to change. Perhaps slowly, and perhaps only in part, but the changes will become apparent in our generations.

Do you want to know how to change your thinking? **Romans 12:2;**
"And do not be conformed to this world, but be transformed by the renewing of your mind, so that you may prove what the will of God is, that which is good and acceptable and perfect." Do not let your mind be controlled by the mass mentality that exists out in the world. Think for yourself and listen to what the true Creator has to tell you. He says in **2 Timothy 2:16;**
"But avoid worldly and empty chatter, for it will lead to further ungodliness," and He tells us this because

He knows how susceptible we are to outward, earthly influence.

Do you want to have that same lifetime contentment, whether in relationships or anything else in your life? It is absolutely attainable, not with a worldly misconception of what it takes, but only with the spiritual instructions that your Manufacturer has provided. Follow the instructions and you will attain both contentment and lasting relationships. De-program yourself from the beliefs of the world, and begin looking in the only instruction manual for humans for your guidance. In it you will find all of the answers that you seek.

At some point in every endeavor you pursue, there will come a testing point; that point to where you have to make the critical decision of whether the reward is worth the cost. If you have never seen the reward, or you don't know the potential reward, as in most relationships, sometimes you are easily swayed by the idle chatter of those around you. Sometimes you will seek answers from those who are still in the same struggle that you are in now; yet they have not attained the reward either, so how can they guide you through that which they do not know to an end that they do not believe in, nor have ever seen?! Seek your guidance and truth where it CAN be found, from

In Pursuit…

someone who HAS already been there. Seek your answers only from those who know.

Contentment comes from the joy you find in every situation and in every relationship. Remember the chapter about Happiness vs. Joy? Joy comes from within. Joy is the result of conscious effort, the decision to see those good and positive things in every situation. Joy is an inside job, and will provide you that contentment. Joy does not equal happiness, nor does contentment. Contentment is one of the results of finding joy. Contentment does not mean stopping your progress towards anything, but exactly the opposite. Contentment enables you to continue to improve yourself and become better at everything you do. It removes the negative perceptions from your life and enables you to become the greatest at all that you do.

This ability to be content is what also enables you to have better relationships with friends, a spouse, family, and even your perceived enemies. It gives you the ability to see beyond the negatives, beyond the disagreements; and allows you to see the opportunities, the positives, and the things that you do love about the person. Being content requires a long learning process. It is a learned behavioral trait that most people do not have, nor will they attain it because it takes time and effort, neither of which are acceptable in an "I want results NOW!" society.

Make the decision to love, to find joy in everyone and everything around you. Look for the joys in every situation and person. Learn to accept the differences and disagreements, and focus on the positive aspects. Look for, remember, and cling to those things about that person that you committed to that made you love them in the beginning of the relationship. Grow with them as you help them grow in their physical and spiritual life. Find contentment, as you are the only person that has control over that aspect of your life. Contentment comes from joy, and that's an inside job. Lasting relationships come from the joy and contentment that are found within them; and that too, my friend, is an inside job.

18 – In Pursuit – Peace & Truth

Sometimes the quest for Truth leads to Peace, but only when that quest ends in finding the Truth. Otherwise, it only leads to frustration, confusion, agitation, or outright anger. Perhaps the quest seems never ending, or at least cumbersome at times, because people are searching for Truth everywhere except where it can be found. "Oh, I've never been there, but I can find it. I don't need any map, and I'm sure not going to stop and ask anyone." Sound familiar… wives? Yep! That's your husband, huh?

You know, I think that those little GPS systems are probably the greatest modern invention yet. All it needs is an address, and boom, you've got directions on how to get anywhere that you want to go. And the wives are saying, "Yeah, great… if I could only get him to turn it on and use it now." It must be a male thing, a direction assistance phobia disease. Men just have this thing about asking directions, don't they? I know. I've got it too! I hate stopping and asking someone for directions. Now, I will occasionally look at a map, but usually only before I leave the house. Once I'm in motion, leave me alone!

Male or female, aren't many of us like that when it comes to seeking the Truth? We want to achieve this great Peace, but we have to find the Truth before we will feel that Peace, yet we just refuse to ask for directions when we go on the great hunt for Truth. So in the end, we are frustrated, confused, agitated, and angry that we didn't find it on our own.

Since you didn't ask for directions and I'm catching you off-guard just a little, I'll offer some directions throughout this chapter, hidden here and there. That way you can get the information you need without losing any of that pride and independence. Truth is what we need here, now, on this earth as long as we are on it and before we are in it. Peace will come from living by the Truth, and will come after life on this earth, after we are in it. That means, forget about Peace until you find the Truth. Focus on finding the Truth first and the Peace will be there when you need it.

The Truth can be a very illusive thing for being so blatantly obvious. Why? Because most people absolutely refuse to seek the Truth where it really is. More and more people will search the well-known talk shows for their Truth; or perhaps some of man's own created theories; or maybe a family member's perspective. So very few will ever search where the

In Pursuit…

Truth lies, primarily due to the simple fact that people are not seeking Truth, but justification. To find Truth means change, and change is quite uncomfortable to most of us. It means a complete change of lifestyle in many cases, and definitely means being questioned by everyone around us as to why we have made these obvious changes. That aspect begins developing a trembling, nauseating fear in most of us. Yet, what are the options?

Well, option number one is to stay just like we are, very self-aware of our unawareness. It means staying purposely away from anything that might even be slightly perceived as even akin to any real Truth. It is a self-inflicted ignorance that some are proud to carry and boast about, as if open and admitted denial will make it somehow cease to exist, thereby justifying any lack of actions to find it. Others may dig a little deeper, but as soon as they stumble onto any part of it, they quickly realize their plunder and throw it out so as not to disturb or inconvenience themselves or their friends. The end result is still denial.

Option number two is to actually find the Truth, and then be faced with the dilemma of whether or not to do anything about it. If you decide to do something about it, then you are committing social suicide, in some cases, unless you completely change those who you spend leisure and work time with. If you decide not to do anything about it, then you have to live with knowledge and the fact that you were too weak to stand up against the untruths. This option is even worse than the denial option. At least in denial you can claim self-inflicted ignorance. Here you are going to hurt either way.

If you seek the Truth, be willing to find it. If you find the Truth, be willing to live by it. If you are willing to live by it, be willing to die for it. Make it that important to you. If you seek justification for yourself, then do not seek the Truth, but only those earthly things and men's ways that will justify you to yourself, for the Truth will not justify you unto yourself, but to God. Only you know what you are truly seeking. Be honest with yourself along the way. Know what it is that you are looking for so that you will follow the right path in finding it. Yet, remember, the Truth is the only right way, and the only way to obtain Peace.

The Truth is in the Bible, and it will require a change in you, but one that you are willing to make if Truth is what you seek. When you find it, you will also find Peace; one that surpasses any like you've

In Pursuit…

ever known before. It will be the Peace that can lead you confidently out of this life and into another realm, the one from whence you came. Truth leads to Peace, and that Peace is eternal life with your Creator.

Don't be mistaken by what the world tells you. You will most certainly have an eternity, the only question is where. One you will be forced to go to; the other you will run willingly to go to. It all depends on whether you truly want to find Truth, or only justification for self. Denial is no excuse. Fear is no excuse. Bad circumstances or a bad childhood or adult life are not excuses, no matter how terrible. Being taken advantage of, being used, or being betrayed are not excuses. Regardless of anything that does or does not happen to you here on this earth, you have no excuse for denying or not knowing or not understanding the Truth. The Bible is your spiritual GPS navigation system. If you choose not to use it or turn it on in your life for any reason at all, that is your choice, just clearly understand this; To God, it will not matter the reason, all that will matter is whether you accepted Him, Loved Him, and listened to Him enough to obey Him. If you deny His Truth, then He also will deny you. If you accept His Truth, He will accept you as one of His children, and you will find the Peace that you long for.

God doesn't ask for anything that you have, just everything that you are. He doesn't force you to love Him, but only pleads with you to. He doesn't ask for your body, only your heart, mind, and soul. If He has those, you will be His in your entirety. God doesn't force you to become His child, but freely offers it to you as He stretches out His arms to welcome you. He doesn't force you to accept His sacrifice, but He offered it up for you anyway in the greatest of hopes that you would accept it. God offered the attainment of joy, contentment, lasting relationships, peace, and truth. He didn't offer you the pursuit of these things, but the attainment of these things. He offers you real treasures, real wealth, and a real reward unlike anything this earth can or will ever be able to offer you.

Stop living 'In Pursuit...", and start living in attainment of His promises. Stop thinking like the herds that believe they are each individual thinkers as they follow the deceived masses. Start thinking like an individual that has a purpose and a backbone to stand against the things that you inherently know are wrong. Stop trying to justify yourself, and start trying to justify yourself to God.

In Pursuit...

Everyone that you know right now is going to die. They will be gone. God will still be there waiting to hear your answer for your actions, or lack of them. How will you answer? What will you say? As you stand before Him, and you will, just as all of us will, you will stand alone to answer to Him. As a child before the Father, you will be held accountable for your life. You will get no second chances, no "do over", and no "I'm sorry. I'll try to do better" will prevent you from your Father's punishment. The ONLY hope you have is offered now, while you are still in this body on this earth, and that hope is believing in and obeying your Savior, Jesus Christ, and following His commands.

Have you ever thought that salvation was like a cafeteria where you can pick and choose the aspects of Jesus you want? "I'll have a little Saviorhood, please, but no Lordship." Not so, friend. If Jesus is not your Lord, Jesus is not your Savior. What's the difference? Well, suppose I perform a wedding ceremony and say to the young man, "Would you take Mary to be your lawfully wedded wife?" and he responds, "Well, I'll take Mary as housekeeper." Then I say to her, "Would you take John to be your lawfully wedded husband?" and she says, "Well, I'll take him as provider." Friend, we can't pick and choose what we want from Jesus. We simply take Jesus as Lord over all!

Is Jesus Christ Lord of every area of your life? Take time today to examine your life, your finances, your relationships, your hopes and dreams. Understand where you are in God's eyes and prepare yourself now.

1 Thessalonians 5:1-3 tells us;
"Now as to the times and the epochs (dates), brethren, you have no need of anything to be written to you. For you yourselves know full well that the day of the Lord will come just like a thief in the night. While they are saying, "Peace and safety!" then destruction will come upon them suddenly like labor pains upon a woman with child, and they will not escape."

Do you know what the problem with many of us is? Our faith is something tacked onto our lives. Instead of guiding our life and being our life, it's just one more thing to keep up with. Jesus said, *"No man can serve two masters..."* (Matthew 6:24). Do you believe that?

You are to have but one goal in your life, and that is to know Jesus Christ personally, powerfully, passionately, and preeminently. Everything else will flow out of that. You say, "But wait a minute. I've got other things to do! I've got a job. I've got to rest. I've got to have recreation. I've got to have friends. I can't just narrow my interests and energy to one thing. I have responsibilities!" When you bring your life into a burning focus for Christ, all of these other things contribute to the main thing and will fall into place accordingly.

The day is coming, whether you are ready or not, and whether you believe or not. You may not believe in God, but He still believes in you. You will meet Him face to face. Again, **Matthew 10:32 & 33** tell us clearly;

"Therefore everyone who confesses Me before men, I will also confess him before My Father who is in heaven. But whoever denies Me before men, I will also deny him before My Father who is in heaven."

Do not be deceived by the tremendous religious disunity that exists today. Do not be deceived by a society that refuses to believe, or even hear. Study, think, and make your own decision based upon the absolute truth of the Bible. No manmade creeds, nor traditions, nor denominations, nor friends or family's opinions, nor any perceived religious leader's words should sway you. They may enlighten you, or inspire you, but never sway you without scriptural backbone. Simply the Word of God, written by divine inspiration should be your only guide. The Bible alone is the human instruction manual. Follow it, and you will discover how to stop pursuing and begin attaining treasures beyond your imagination; treasures laid up in Heaven where nothing can destroy or decay them.

In Pursuit…

<u>19 - So, Where Does The Peace Come From?</u>
Repenting

As Christians, we often talk about the <u>Plan of Salvation</u>. We will discuss some of that here, and more in the final chapter. So that you will understand a little more about it, you need to consider exactly what that plan really means, and what it is, and where the Peace that you so desperately seek really comes from out of all of this.

Jesus told Nicodemus in **John 3.7, "You must be born again."** Yet, what does this new birth require? Let's overview God's Plan, with special emphasis on Repentance and what that really means.

In today's confused culture of so many different churches and beliefs, how do you know the right way? The only way or plan to be followed is God's way (God's Plan) for salvation. That way is simple to understand, yet so often misunderstood.

People who claim the name of "Christians" worldwide have discounted salvation into a quick-fix, convenience oriented, emotional moment of guilt, where we momentarily feel some guilt, and accept no further responsibility; yet no continual change and spiritual maturity to follow. It is taught by many denominations and in our own non-denominational brotherhood of Bible believing churches that we are "saved" by a simple acknowledgement of believing in God and in Jesus as His Son, or a simple "sinner's prayer"; then Grace just kind of follows us around covering all the rest of our life's "mistakes." ("Mistakes", because we don't want to talk too much about "saved" people's "sins" and make them feel uncomfortable.)

How completely opposite from scripture could those that teach such "salvation" be?!

We need to better understand what God's Plan really is, straight from the Bible, and what **Repent** truly means in our spiritual journey, in order to grow ourselves, and to assure that we are teaching true Salvation to others in this confused and blind age.

You can only understand if you take ALL of the scripture together, in context. Taking *this* verse here and *that* verse there and trying to establish God's Plan from just one or two passages is NOT going to give you the complete plan that God Himself designed. So study it all.

In Pursuit…

Most of us have heard or read the Plan of Salvation, in short;
Hear, Believe, Repent, Confess, Be Baptized.

Hearing involves hearing the Word, the Gospel specifically; **"How shall they call on him whom they have not believed? And how shall they believe him whom they have not heard? And how shall they hear without a preacher?" (Romans 10:14).** There are many other passages that support Hearing as well.

And *Believing* involves just that… Believing that what you Hear about and from the Bible is true, and most specifically about Jesus and His life, death, and resurrection. **"And without faith it is impossible to be well pleasing unto him; for he that cometh to God must believe that he is, and that he is a rewarder of them that seek after him" (Hebrews 11:6).** Again, there are many passages that speak about Believing.

We'll come back to *Repent* in just a moment…

Confessing, which we also study about in scripture and have solid scriptural support for, is also simple to understand. It is the Confessing with the lips that you believe Jesus, our Savior and Christ, is the Son of the One True & Living God.

- By example; **"Behold here is water; What doth hinder me to be baptized ? And Philip said, if thou believeth with all thy heart thou mayest. And he answered and said, I believe that Jesus Christ is the Son of God" (Acts 8:36-37).**

- Also by direct command; Jesus said, **"If you will confess me before men, I will confess you before my father." Matthew 10.32.** Being a disciple of Jesus demands a confession.Also, **Romans 10.9** tells us that **"with the mouth confession is made unto salvation."** Jesus insisted upon a confession.

Baptize… well, although debated about among the so-called theological scholars, scripture clearly states Be Baptized for the remission of sins. **"And Peter said unto them, Repent ye, and be baptized everyone of you in the name of Jesus Christ unto the remission of your sins and ye shall receive the gift of the Holy Spirit" (Acts 2:38).**There are many other scriptures, as well, that clearly make the command for us, not as a work, but as an act of Faith, to be baptized for the forgiveness of our sins.
Sins are forgiven in baptism. Baptism is for the remission of sins.

In Pursuit…

The word **baptize** comes from the Greek word "baptizo" and literally means, **"to dip, to immerse, to plunge."** In addition to the literal meaning of the word, immersion is practiced because it was the practice of the church in apostolic times. Still further, only immersion conforms to the description of baptism as given by the apostle Paul in **Romans 6:3-6** where he speaks of it as a burial and resurrection, as well as this new birth.

The word **"baptizo"** occurs **86** times in the Greek KJV (from Matthew 3:6 - Luke 12:50). This word should not be confused with the Greek word *baptô*. The clearest example that shows the meaning of **baptizo** is a text from the Greek poet and physician Nicander, who lived about 200 B.C. It is in a recipe for making pickles and is helpful because it uses both words. Nicander says that in order to make a pickle, the vegetable should first be **'dipped'** (*baptô*) into boiling water and then **'baptized'** (*baptizô*) in the vinegar solution. Both verbs concern the <u>immersing</u> of vegetables in a solution. But the first (*baptô*) is temporary. The second (*baptizô*), the act of **baptizing** the vegetable, <u>produces a permanent change</u>. The significance to you? Simply this…Being **Baptized** (*baptizô*) is an act of Faith that <u>causes a permanent change</u>.

When you are immersed in water, that is, Baptized for the forgiveness of your past sins, **"ye shall receive the gift of the Holy Spirit" (Acts 2:38)** which clearly states that this receiving of the Holy Spirit follows **baptism.**

Our faith must then cause us to Diligently seek Him. With the Holy Spirit acting as our comfort along this continual journey as we traverse every terrain, we can realign our lives by following the compass, Jesus, who always points us to God.

Now, *REPENT*. What does this really mean?

Repentance is a most difficult command to obey. But Jesus said, **"Except you repent, you shall all likewise perish."**Peter on Pentecost answered those who had killed The Christ, **"Repent and be baptized."**Then in Acts 3.19, he says, **"Repent and be converted."**

Diligently seeking God means that we must be willing to turn (**Repent**) from our life of sin and serving self and serve Him.

In Pursuit…

We see the word **"repent"** in the Hebrew and Greek forms in the Bible. A few interesting points:·

- The Hebrew form *nacham* (nä·kham') occurs **108** times in the Hebrew KJV (from Genesis 5:29 – 2 Sam. 24:16), and it literally means;
- **1)** to be sorry, be moved to pity, have compassion·
- **2)** to be sorry, rue, suffer grief, repent·
- The Greek form *metanoeō* (me-tä-no-e'-ō), occurs **36** times in the Greek KJV (from Matthew 3:2 – Rev. 2:21), and it literally means;
- **1)** to change one's mind (heart) for better, heartily to amend with abhorrence of one's past sins·
- The Greek form *metanoia* (me-tä'-noi-ä), occurs **24** times in the Greek KJV (from Matthew 3:8 – 2 Peter 3:9), which literally means;
- **1)** a change of mind (heart) of a purpose he has formed or of something he has done
- Hebrew form is **All Old Testament.**·
- Greek forms are **All New Testament. (**The Greek translation is said to have been used because it was a "dead" language, and the logic was that

since it was a "dead" (unused) language, it would never change.

Now HERE, is an amazing example of the Purity and everlasting, untainted Truth of the inspiration of God's Word...From the Hebrew form **nacham**, to the Greek forms *metanoeō and metanoia...To the Anglo-French form **repentir**, to the Medieval Latin form **repoenitēre**,To the Latin form **repaenitēre**, To our English form today **repent**... The definitive meaning has remained throughout so many cultures and millennia...<u>**UNCHANGED!**</u>*

The definition of **repent** today, according to Merriam-Webster Dictionary online is:·
- **1)** to turn from sin and dedicate oneself to the amendment of one's life
- **2)** to feel regret or contrition
- **3)** to change one's mind (heart)
- **4)** to feel deep sorrow

Here's where I believe that so many people get confused about **Repentance** and what it really means.

Admitting your sin is NOT **repenting**, it's nothing more than admission and confession of sins.

195

In Pursuit…

Feeling sorry about those sins is NOT **repenting**, it's only regret, and sometimes only regret that you got caught.

True **repentance** only happens at the point of Brokenness, out of deep Anguish, a Sorrow so deep that it breaks your heart to the point of action.

True **repentance** is a sorrowful and grieving process that brings about COMPLETE change in your heart.

True **repentance** is a point where selfishness turns completely over to selflessness.

It is when you realign your life… your thoughts, your actions, your words, your everything…Where your life is 100% realigned to God's will and God's purpose…Not just away from your own desires and goals, but to where your desires and goals ARE God's for you.

So, you **Hear**; you **Believe**; then you **Repent** BECAUSE you **Believe**… you feel regret, sorrow, you are moved to pity, and suffer grief over your current condition. You are SO moved and suffering

SUCH deep grief, that you know you MUST turn from sin and dedicate yourself to amend your life, change it by changing your mind, your heart, from the way you have been living; to change your mind and heart for better; heartily to amend your life with abhorrence of your past sins.

THAT is why you **Confess**, and THAT **REPENTANCE** is why you want to be **Baptized** for the Forgiveness of those sins that separate you from God, and to continue walking in the Light.

And THAT kind of **Repenting** is what makes you Diligently Seek God and His will in your life.

It takes the grief and sorrow of knowing where you are and where you are going in sin, to understand and follow where you can be in Christ.

And THAT kind of **Repenting** is what will bring you the **Peace** in your life that you so desperately seek.

In Pursuit…

20 – The Attainment of Atonement - The Plan

Where will you be on that day, and how will you answer to the God that rolls the skies back as a scroll?

There are so many religions out there... How do I know who or what is really right? How do I be just a Christian? In this time of religious disunity, is it possible to be just Christians today? There is a different church on every corner, so who's right?!

The Bible is the ONLY authority that has the Plan of your Salvation. No man-made creeds, simply God's Word alone.

What the Bible teaches about the Plan of Salvation in the New Testament

God's Simple Plan To Save Man:

1. You Must HEAR the Gospel Message. Romans 10:9 & 17

2. You Must BELIEVE In Jesus Christ. John 8:32

3. You Must REPENT of Your Sins. Luke 13:3
Repenting is difficult, and is born out of Anguish and
Brokenness.
4. You Must CONFESS Faith in Christ. Matthew
10:32

5. You Must Be BAPTIZED (immersed) for the
Forgiveness of Sins. Acts 2:38 & 22:16
As an act of faith you are then BAPTIZED for the
Forgiveness of your past Sins, that have seperated you
from God.

6. You Must LIVE FAITHFULLY. Revelation 2:10
We do not then claim perfection as human beings.
Our only perfection is found in the fact that we have
been forgiven by the blood of Christ as we strive to
walk in the Light.

Now, let's take a little closer look at what the
Bible teaches about each of these steps to your
salvation, using only the Bible as our guide.

In Pursuit…
A Closer Look at God's Plan

Only follow Jesus, using only the Bible as your instruction and guide… no man-made creeds or other doctrine created by men.

The followers of Christ were first called disciples, *"And the word of God increased; and the number of disciples multiplied in Jerusalem greatly."* **Acts 6:7**. When the word of God is proclaimed to people of honest hearts, the result is always disciples. We must return to discipleship in our churches….Simply following Jesus.

Later the followers of the resurrected Jesus were called *"those of the way"* in **Acts 9:2**. The followers had a discipline, a method, a road, a *way* to travel. Following Christ demands a ***way of life***. Simply claiming to be a follower does not make an individual one. There is a plan, a creed, a discipline, a doctrine to be followed if we are to be his disciple. We believe this *way* to be found only in the Bible. It must be our only creed.

In fact, we are warned NOT to follow men's creeds. We are warned about this in **Mark 7:7-9**;

"BUT IN VAIN DO THEY WORSHIP ME, TEACHING AS DOCTRINES THE PRECEPTS OF MEN. Neglecting the commandment of God, you hold to the tradition of men." He was also saying to them, "You are experts at setting aside the commandment of God in order to keep your tradition."

We see in this, and can see in other supporting passages, that following any manmade creeds are not acceptable worship. This means that following a denominational creed formulated by men, for whatever reason, is not what God wants of us.

Then in **Acts 11.26** we find this statement, *"And the disciples were called Christians first in Antioch."* The word means... *One who follows... One who belongs to.* A Christian then is one who <u>follows</u> or <u>belongs</u> to Christ, plain and simple.

Yes, it is possible to be just Christians today. The basis is simple*:*

Are we following Christ? Do we belong to Christ? If so, we are Christians.

What we should believe is laid out plainly before us:

In Pursuit…

We need to believe the Bible when it teaches that we are all saved by grace through faith in Christ. *"God raised us up with Christ and seated us with him in the heavenly realms in Christ Jesus, in order that in the coming ages he might show the incomparable riches of his grace, expressed in his kindness to us in Christ Jesus. For it is by grace you have been saved, through faith--and this not from yourselves, it is the gift of God--not by works, so that no-one can boast. For we are God's workmanship, created in Christ Jesus to do good works, which God prepared in advance for us to do"*. **Ephesians 2:6-10.**

We need to believe that we maintain our salvation through striving to walk in the Light. *"If we walk in the light, as he is in the light, we have fellowship with one another, and the blood of Jesus, his Son, continues to cleanse us from all sin."* **1 John 1:7.**

How To Be Just Christians:

Jesus told Nicodemus in John 3.7, *"You must be born again."* The only *way* or plan to be followed is God's *way* (God's Plan) for salvation. That *way* is simple.

• **We must acknowledge our sins.** We are sinners. There is no chance to be saved until this condition is admitted.

"There is none righteous, no not one... For all have sinned and come short of the glory of God." **Romans 3.10 & 23.**

"For the wages of sin is death." **Romans 6.23.**

We must not trust in our feelings, in the advice of our neighbors; but trust only in the Word of God. Are we willing?

We must believe in Him. *"Without faith it is impossible to please him. For he that comes to God must believe that he is, and that he is a rewarder of them that diligently seek him."* **Hebrews 6:11.**

Our faith must cause us to *Diligently seek him.* Repentance is a most difficult command to obey. But Jesus said, *"Except you repent, you shall all likewise perish."*

Peter on Pentecost answered those who had killed The Christ. *"Repent and be baptized."*

Then in **Acts 3:19**, he says, *"Repent and be converted."*

In Pursuit…

Diligently seeking God means that we must be willing to turn from our life of sin and serving self and turn (Repent) and serve him.

Jesus insisted upon a confession. He said, *"If you will confess me before men, I will confess you before my father."* **Matthew 10:32.** Being a disciple of Jesus demands a confession. Too many today call themselves Christians, but by their confession it is obvious they are not. **Romans 10:9** tells us that *"with the mouth confession is made unto salvation."*

Sins are forgiven in baptism. Baptism is not for church membership, not because we are already saved people, or to satisfy our family or friends. Baptism is for the remission of sins.

In **Acts 2:38**, Peter said two things were required before sins could be remitted and the Holy Spirit could be given. *"Repent and be Baptized."*

Paul in relating the events surrounding his conversion experience in Acts 22 made this statement concerning his baptism. *"And now why tarriest thou? Arise and be baptized, and wash away thy sins, calling on the name of the Lord."* **Acts 22:16.**

Romans 6:4-6 gives us some details about this new birth. Baptism is the crucifixion of the man of sin and the resurrection to a new beginning in Christ. *"We are buried with him by baptism into death: That like as Christ was raised up from the dead by the glory of the Father, even so we also should walk in newness of life. For as we have been planted together in the likeness of his death, we shall be also in the likeness of his resurrection: Knowing this, that our old man is crucified with him, that the body of sin might be destroyed, that henceforth we should not serve sin."*

In baptism we become children of God by faith. *"For we are all the children of God by faith in Christ Jesus. For as many of you as have been baptized into Christ have put on Christ. (Have been clothed with Christ)."* **Galatians 3:26-27.**

You must be buried with Christ and born again.

Our plea is that men everywhere realize that we are all sinners; believe in God and the sacrifice of Jesus as His son; diligently seek Him through repentance and confession of His name; put on Christ, be clothed with His righteousness, in the act of New Testament baptism.

The church is an outward manifestation of the deep conviction in our hearts that Christianity is

In Pursuit…

produced today by the same *Living Word of God* which produced Christians in the New Testament.

We do not claim perfection as human beings. Our only perfection is found in the fact that we have been forgiven by the blood of Christ as we strive to walk in the Light. We are all sinners saved by grace through faith.

Our aim is to glorify God by exalting Christ in our daily walk and teaching... *To Be Christians Only.*

Through **hearing, believing, confessing, repenting, and being baptized** into Christ, you can begin the Christian walk. It is a battle that requires constant vigil against the desires of this fleshly body and the sinful nature that we have all been born into. Becoming a Christian does NOT mean that life becomes easier, but on the contrary, life becomes much more difficult as you constantly engage in spiritual battle. Jesus Himself told us that when we become Christians, followers of Him, that we will face persecution and strife because of Him. So understand the army in which you enlist, and be prepared to defend the Word and honor of your Savior.

Walk the walk, talk the talk, and run the race. The reward is greater than any of us can perceive. But if you will follow Him, the victory and the reward are assured, and no one or nothing can take that away from you.

Ephesians 2:8 & 9;

"For by grace you have been saved through faith; and that not of yourselves, it is the gift of God; not as a result of works, so that no one may boast."

Mark 16:15 & 16;

"And He said to them, "Go into all the world and preach the gospel to all creation. He who has believed and has been baptized shall be saved; but he who has disbelieved shall be condemned."

James 5:15-20;

"And the prayer offered in faith will restore the one who is sick, and the Lord will raise him up, and if he has committed sins, they will be forgiven him.

Therefore, confess your sins to one another, and pray for one another so that you may be healed. The effective prayer of a righteous man can accomplish much.

In Pursuit…
Elijah was a man with a nature like ours, and he prayed earnestly that it would not rain, and it did not rain on the earth for three years and six months. Then he prayed again, and the sky poured rain and the earth produced its fruit.

My brethren, if any among you strays from the truth and one turns him back, let him know that he who turns a sinner from the error of his way will save his soul from death and will cover a multitude of sins."

Use the Jesus as your compass, not the clock of the world. Stop pursuing Peace, Happiness, & Contentment in worldly places and ways; attain them all through God in Christ and start making a Life Forever, not just a living for this life.
We have been given an instruction manual, a map to get us to the end goal…
It's called, the Bible. Use it; Live by it; Discover God's Absolute Truth and the Peace that comes from it; & MAY GOD BLESS YOU forever!
Amen.

www.ingramcontent.com/pod-product-compliance
Lightning Source LLC
Chambersburg PA
CBHW061405280526
45784CB00001B/380